Giuseppe Verdi

La Forza del Destino

(The Power of Fate, or The Force of Destiny)

OPERA STUDY GUIDE

AND

LIBRETTO

OPERA CLASSICS LIBRARY™ SERIES

Edited by Burton D. Fisher
Principal lecturer, *Opera Journeys Lecture Series*

Opera Journeys™ Publishing / Boca Raton, Florida

WEB SITE: www.operajourneys.com E MAIL: operaj@bellsouth.net

Contents

Opera Journeys™ Mini Guide Series

Opera Classics Library™ Series

Opera Journeys™ Libretto Series

A History of Opera: Milestones and Metamorphoses

Mozart's Da Ponte Operas

PUCCINI COMPANION

Verdi Companion: 27 Opera Study Guide

Over 125 GUIDES & LIBRETTI AVAILABLE: Print or Ebook

•The Abduction from the Seraglio •Adriana Lecouvreur •L'Africaine •Aida •Andrea Chénier •Anna Bolena •Ariadne auf Naxos •Armida •Attila •The Ballad of Baby Doe •The Barber of Seville •Duke Bluebeard's Castle •La Bohème •Boris Godunov •Candide •Capriccio •Carmen •Cavalleria Rusticana •Cendrillon •La Cenerentola •La Clemenza di Tito •Le Comte Ory •Così fan tutte •The Crucible •La Damnation de Faust •The Death of Klinghoffer •Doctor Atomic •Don Carlo •Don Giovanni •Don Pasquale •La Donna del Lago •The Elixir of Love •Elektra •Ernani •Eugene Onegin •Exploring Wagner's Ring •Falstaff •La Fanciulla del West •Faust •La Fille du Régiment •Fidelio •Die Fledermaus •The Flying Dutchman •Die Frau ohne Schatten •Der Freischütz •Gianni Schicchi •La Gioconda •Hamlet •Hansel and Gretel •Henry VIII •Iolanta •L'Italiana in Algeri •Les Huguenots •Iphigénie en Tauride •Julius Caesar •Lakmé •Lohengrin •Lucia di Lammermoor •Macbeth •Madama Butterfly •The Magic Flute •The Makropolis Case •Manon •Manon Lescaut •Maria Stuarda •The Marriage of Figaro •A Masked Ball •Die Meistersinger •The Mikado •Nabucco •Nixon in China •Norma •Of Mice and Men •Orfeo ed Euridice •Otello •I Pagliacci •Parsifal •The Pearl Fishers •Pelléas et Mélisande •Porgy and Bess •Prince Igor •I Puritani •The Queen of Spades •The Rake's Progress •The Rape of Lucretia •The Rhinegold •Rigoletto •The Ring of the Nibelung •Roberto Devereaux •Rodalinda •Roméo et Juliette •La Rondine •Der Rosenkavalier •Rusalka •Salome •Samson and Delilah •Show Boat •Siegfried •Simon Boccanegra •La Sonnambula •Suor Angelica •Susannah •Il Tabarro •The Tales of Hoffmann •Tannhäuser •Thaïs •Tosca •La Traviata •Tristan and Isolde •Il Trittico •Les Troyens •Il Trovatore •Turandot •The Valkyrie •Werther •West Side Story •Wozzeck

WWW.OPERAJOURNEYS.COM

a *Prelude........*

OPERA CLASSICS LIBRARY's *La Forza del Destino* STUDY GUIDE AND LIBRETTO

There exists a host of artistic creations that dwell on fate and curses, but few capture the dramatic impact of Verdi's *La Forza del Destino,* a story that can be as confounding as its music is compelling.

Like "Fate" itself, the inherent power of Verdi's score is undeniable. Cruel destiny separates father from daughter, brother from sister, and the intense passions of two young lovers. The melodrama becomes intensified by the curse of a dying father, a blood feud, hate, sword duels, and the all-consuming passions of revenge and retribution.

Verdi's magnificent musical inventions transform a rather perplexing and disquieting melodrama into one of the most compelling and turbulent works for the lyric theater: the opera is saturated with a rich abundance of melodic invention and colorful and mature harmonic development.

But love and betrayal dominate the interplay of passions of *La Forza del Destino*'s protagonists: all represent aspects of powerless humanity, victimized by the incomprehensible forces of "fate" and "destiny."

OPERA CLASSICS LIBRARY explores the greatness of Verdi's La Forza del Destino. The *Commentary and Analysis* offers pertinent biographical information about Verdi, his mind-set at the time of *La Forza*'s composition, the genesis of the opera, its premiere and performance history, and insightful and in depth story and character analysis.

The text also contains a *Brief Story Synopsis, Principal Characters in La Forza,* and a *Story Narrative with Music Highlight Examples,* the latter containing original music transcriptions that are interspersed within the story's dramatic exposition. In addition, the text includes a *Dictionary of Opera and Musical Terms.*

The *Libretto* provides the translation in a side-by-side format, and also contains musical highlight examples interspersed within the drama's text.

The opera art form is the sum of many artistic expressions: theatrical drama, music, scenery, poetry, dance, acting and gesture. In opera, it is the composer who is the dramatist, using the emotive power of his music and the kinetic intensity of the prose to provide powerful theater, an impact on one's sensibilities that can reach into the very depths of the human soul.

Verdi's *La Forza del Destino* is a crown jewel among Verdi's glorious operatic inventions: it remains a masterpiece of the lyric theater as well as a tribute to the art form.

Burton D. Fisher
Editor
OPERA CLASSICS LIBRARY

La Forza del Destino

(The Power of Fate, or The Force of Destiny)

Opera in Italian in four acts

Music
by
Giuseppe Verdi

Libretto by Francesco Maria Piave,
after *Don Álvaro, o la fuerza del sino* (1835),
a drama by Spanish playwright Angel de Saavedra, 3rd Duke of Rivas;
with elements of Friedrich Schiller's *Wallensteins Lager,*
adapted by Andrea Maffei.

Premiere: November 1862,
Bolshoi Kamenny (Imperial) Theatre, St. Petersburg, Russia

Revised: February 27, 1869, premiere at La Scala, Milan.
A new *Overture* replaced the original *Prelude*;
a new final scene for Act III,
following the duel between Carlo and Álvaro;
and a new conclusion in which Álvaro remains alive
at the conclusion of the opera.

Commentary and Analysis

By the mid-point of the nineteenth century, Giuseppe Verdi had become the bearer of the mantle of the most popular opera composer in the world: he had become an icon whose operas were the box office rage in Italy, Europe, and throughout the world.

Voice, song and melody remained the quintessential core of Verdi's musical inventions, as the composer dutifully preserved the great legacy, traditions and conventions of Rossini, Bellini and Donizetti, the bel canto masters who had preceded him.

At mid-century, the European opera landscape was indeed sparse: Rossini had retired 20-years earlier; Bellini died in 1835; and Donizetti died in 1848. The only significant works for the lyric theater were Meyerbeer's *Le Prophète* premiered in 1849; and Wagner's *Lohengrin* in 1850.

It seemed that Verdi was the only active opera composer capable of mesmerizing audiences and capturing their romantic imagination. Between 1839 and 1850, he composed 15 operas, *Oberto* (1839), his first opera, indicated promise for the young 26-year-old budding opera composer. But his second opera, the comedy *Un Giorno di Regno* (1840), was received with indifference and ultimately deemed a total failure.

Nabucco (1842), Verdi's third opera, was a sensational triumph that catapulted Verdi to immediate world-wide critical and popular acclaim. Verdi followed with one success after another: *I Lombardi* (1843); *Ernani* (1844); *I Due Foscari* (1844); *Giovanna d'Arco* (1845); *Alzira* (1845); *Attila* (1846); *Macbeth* (1847); *I Masnadieri* (1847); *Il Corsaro* (1848); *La Battaglia di Legnano* (1849); *Luisa Miller* (1849); and *Stiffelio* (1850).

Significantly, Verdi used his operatic pen to sound the alarm for Italy's freedom: almost all the underlying stories of his early operas addressed the composer's all-consuming patriotic mission for the liberation of Italy from oppressive foreign rule, in particular, that of Austria. Those opera scenarios were disguised in allegory, which ennobled the ideals of individual liberty, freedom and national independence — the suffering and struggling heroes and heroines of Verdi's early operas were symbolically his beloved Italian compatriots.

In *Nabucco,* the biblical story of Nebuchadnezzar, the suffering Hebrews were exiled and enslaved by the Babylonians; allegorically, they were the Italian people, similarly victims of foreign oppression. Verdi's Italian audience easily grasped his idealistic call for Italian independence, a theme that was subtly injected between the lines of the libretto text and nobly expressed through Verdi's musical language.

At *Nabucco*'s premiere, at the conclusion of the Hebrew exile chorus, "Va, pensiero, sull'ali dorata" ("Fly, thought, on golden wings"), the audience stopped the performance for fifteen minutes with wild shouts of "Viva Italia" — it was an explosion of nationalistic fervor that provoked the authorities to assign extra police to later performances of the opera in order to prevent riots. Verdi's "Va, pensiero" became the emotional and unofficial "Italian National Anthem" — a musical expression of Italy's aspirations for independence.

As the 1850s unfolded, Verdi's creative genius had arrived at a turning point in terms of his artistic goals and objectives. He felt satisfied that his mission to achieve Italian independence was soon to be realized, and indeed, the *Risorgimento* (1861) liberated Italy from foreign rule and established the Italian nation.

At this juncture, Verdi decided to abandon the heroic pathos and nationalistic fervor of his early operas. His new goal was to seek more profound operatic subjects: subjects that were bold to the extreme; subjects with greater dramatic and psychological depth; subjects that accented spiritual values, intimate humanity, tender emotions — and as towering passions.

The year 1851 inaugurated what Verdi scholars have designated as his "middle period" — a defining moment in his musico-dramatic maturity in which his operatic oeuvre began to contain heretofore unknown dramatic qualities: a profound characterization of humanity integrated with an exceptionally visceral lyricism. During this period, Verdi's art matured and flowered, and his lyric theater works became some of the best loved works: *Rigoletto* (1851); *Il Trovatore* (1853); *La Traviata* (1853); *I Vespri Siciliani* (1855); *Simon Boccanegra* (1857); *Aroldo* (1857); *Un Ballo in Maschera* (1859); *La Forza del Destino* (1862); *Don Carlos* (1867); and *Aïda* (1871).

After the great success of *Aïda*, it would have seemed appropriate that the 58-year-old Verdi would acknowledge that he had reached the twilight of an extremely prolific opera-composing career — a time when he was supposed to be relishing his golden years, and a time when the fires of ambition were supposed to have extinguished —the time when most people become spectators in the show of life rather than its stars. However, Verdi decided to defy the natural order and adopt as his mantra the words of Robert Browning's Rabbi Ben Ezra: "Grow old along with me! The best is yet to be!"

Consequently, Verdi overturned the equation and transformed his old age into creating works that became the crowning glory of his career: two operatic masterpieces — *Otello* (1887) and *Falstaff* (1893) — that many Verdian aficionados consider the tours-de-force of Italian opera. Both operas were unprecedented in the Italian lyric theater; both operas highlight a continuity and integrity of textual and musical elements, and ideal of the lyric drama which sought dramatic truth — the kinetic power of the text, combined with the emotive power of music.

Verdi died in 1901 at the age of 88.

"Destiny" and/or "Fate" are traditionally defined as a power or agency that has a predetermined sequence or course of events conceived to occur in the future; it defines events that are either "ordered" or "inevitable" and/or "unavoidable."

Although often used interchangeably, "fate" and "destiny" contain distinct connotations: the defining concept suggests the belief that there is a fixed natural order of the universe and the cosmos.

"Fate" is often conceived as a divinely inspired event. Classical and European mythology featured personified "fate spinners." such as the Moirai in Greek mythology; the Parcase Roman mythology, and the Norns in Norse mythology. The "fate spinners" determined the events of the world through a mystical form of spinning of thread — the thread representing individual human "fate."

"Destiny" occurs without regard to the finality of events, or to the process through which events become manifested. There is a sense of "destination" or conclusion — a wherewithal of the flow of events as they are manifested.

"Fatalism" refers to the belief that events fixed by "fate" are unchangeable through human agency. In other words, humans can have no effect(s) upon their own "fate" or upon the "fate" of others.

"Fate" "Destiny" "Lot" "Portion" and "Doom" define a predetermined state or end. "Fate" implies an inevitable and usually adverse outcome, e.g., "the fate of the ship is futile."

"Destiny" implies something foreordained and often suggests a great nobility as it seeks conclusion: e.g., "the country's destiny is to be a model of freedom to the world."

"Lot" and "Portion" imply a distribution through "fate" or "destiny": "Lot" suggests blind chance, such as, "it was her lot to die childless" and "Portion" implies the apportioning of good and evil, such as, "remorse that has become his daily "portion."

"Doom" distinctly implies a grim or calamitous "fate," e.g., "if the rebellion fails, "doom" is certain.

"Fate" and "Destiny" represent significant underlying philosophies within Western culture's "Greek connection." In the classic Greek drama of *Electra*, each of the Greek playwrights — Aeschylus, Euripedes and Sophocles — related the same fundamental story involving Electra's consuming obsession for violence and hateful revenge. But each dramatist used the heroine's specific tragedy as a forum to speculate about man's responsibility for his actions: Are there gods or providential powers controlling human actions? Or, are all human actions the result of fate or chance?

In Aeschylus's trilogy of the *Oresteia*, the central character Orestes, the son of Agamemnon, who has now grown to manhood and has returned to claim his rightful kingdom. He recognizes his sister Electra among the serving women and becomes emboldened by justice: avenging the crime by killing his mother and her paramour.

However, after the deed, Orestes becomes conflicted: he believes that he acted justly and according to the wishes of Apollo, the god of prophecy and reason. But he simultaneously shatters under the emotional strain of his guilt, and imagines the avenging gods pursuing him because he caused family blood to spill. Eventually, Athena, the goddess of wisdom, rescues the soul of Orestes and restores his sanity by removing evil from the world.

In Aeschylus's *Oresteia*, the tragic conflict is resolved by the intervention of the god's higher truth: the gods emerge as omnipotent powers consumed to teach humanity justice and prescribe moral codes for human action.

Euripedes dramatized the pathological nature of the drama of obsessive revenge by shifting the sympathy away from the siblings, Orestes and Electra, and condemning the gods for allowing such incomprehensible and horrible acts to occur. Therefore, the gods are deemed destructive and the cause of the tragedy by inflicting their capricious wills on defenseless humanity. Euripides viewed the gods with irony and ambivalence, and concluded that if they existed at all they were impotent — a mere projection of fears and desires evolving from humanity's collective unconscious and/or his imagination. Euripedes suggested that if indeed the gods existed, they were evil; and if the gods did not exist, man's destiny was ordained by mere chance.

Sophocles built upon Euripedes's conception of random incidence by stressing that all human destiny resulted from uncontrollable fate. In the drama of Electra, she becomes Sophocles's central character: a once beautiful young woman full of love and tenderness, who becomes transformed into savagery, by her all-consuming obsession to avenge her father's murder.

Electra hears news that her brother Orestes dead, but she is unaware that the event was false news spread by Orestes himself in order to gain access to the palace and fulfill the "holy" deed. After trying unsuccessfully to enlist the help of her sister, Chrysothemis, Electra decides to exact vengeance herself. While she frantically digs for the axe, a disguised stranger appears and presents her with an urn that supposedly contains Orestes's ashes. Moved by her grief, the stranger realizes that he has found his sister and proceeds to reveal his true identity. Orestes immediately enters the palace and slays his mother, Clytemnestra, and her paramour, Aegisthus.

Sophocles stark version of the drama portrays Electra as a woman incensed and driven into savagery by her monomania for revenge; but Sophocles also endows her with qualities of heroism and tragic endurance. Electra expresses an entire range of human emotions: she alternates between passionate love for her brother, sister and father, and cruel hatred of her mother, to numb despair at the news of Orestes's death. She is overwhelmed by joy and ecstasy after Orestes returns and learning that the avenging deed has been fulfilled. Sophocles portrays Electra as mentally and emotionally distraught: a woman incurably disturbed by her all-consuming obsessive passions of hatred and revenge.

In Sophocles, the tragic events occur because of human moral weakness: the gods are nonexistent, indifferent and distant. Humanity possesses no providential powers in the universe — man lives in dark ignorance and becomes a helpless pawn of incomprehensible and uncontrollable forces. Electra — not the gods — precipitates the horrifying tragedy. She is the unwitting victim not of the gods, but of the natural forces of evil in the universe. However, in the end, virtue and justice are triumphant: with the deaths of Electra, Clytemnestra and Aegisthus, harmony has been restored because fatal evil forces have been removed,enabling the universe to be reconciled.

In antiquity, the natural sequel to the Electra tragedy was that Orestes paid the penalty for his offense against moral law — and as a result the Furies pursued him, unabated and unmercifully.

By its very nature, genius tends to be manifested in strange, incomprehensible, and at times mysterious ways.

After the premiere of *Un Ballo in Maschera* (1859) Verdi had reached a compositional hiatus in which he was seeking renewed energy and creative inspiration. But Verdi had become depressed and disillusioned by the state of the opera art form. Beginning at the mid-nineteenth century — Italian opera's golden age had become tarnished. Certainly, the passionate intensity that inspired the German philosopher, Friedrich Nietzsche, to refer to Italian musical expression as the "Mediterranean" soul of music seemed to have lost much of its fiery inspiration.

And there is no doubt that Verdi was subconsciously affected by the Wagnerian affliction that had invaded the opera-world: that many of Wagner's precepts were making a major impact on what the maestro considered the "holy" conventions and traditions of Italian opera.

Coinciding with the premiere of *Un Ballo in Maschera,* Verdi had become a revered national figure. At the personal insistence of Count Camillo de Cavour, who Verdi referred to as "the father of our country," the maestro agreed to serve as a deputy in the newly formed Italian parliament.

Verdi's accomplishments in the lyric theater were directly related to his achievements as an Italian patriot. In many instances the nationalistic themes that were deeply embedded as metaphors in Verdi's early operas expressed the patriotic soul of the composer as well as those of his Italian compatriots. VERDI — Viva Vittorio Emanuele Re d'Italia — had become an acrostic representing Italian national aspirations, particularly during early 1861, the first shaky months of Italian statehood and independence.

Verdi was 46-years-old after the premiere of *Un Ballo in Maschera.* He began to dramatically announce to his friends that his priority had now become tending to his farmlands at S. Agata, which had now demanded much of his time. But retirement seemed to be idle talk, because the fires of Verdi's creative inspiration never waned and he was not quite ready to put down his operatic pen.

With *Un Ballo in Maschera* the maestro had composed twenty-one operas, eighteen of them since the premiere of *Nabucco* in 1842. He would often refer to that post-*Nabucco* period as his "sixteen years in the galley" — a claim that suggested that during that lengthy period he had never enjoyed a moment of peace.

However, in the remaining forty years of Verdi's life, he would compose five operas, perhaps his greatest works: *La Forza del Destino* (which premiered in 1862 and was revised in 1869); *Don Carlos* (1867); and *Aida* (1871). And during Verdi's final creative period he composed *Otello* (1887) and *Falstaff* (1893).

The commission for the first of Verdi's last five operas, *La Forza del Destino*, was proposed by the Imperial Theatre in St. Petersburg, an idea supposedly masterminded by the renowned Enrico Tamberlik, a "tenore robusto" who eventually sang Don Álvaro at *La Forza*'s premiere. Additional spice was provided by the Russian government, who assured Verdi that its public adored the Maestro. Giuseppina, now Verdi's wife, was enthralled by the prospect of visiting Russia.

Historically, Russians adored Italian opera. The art form had been a consuming passion after it received its greatest impetus from Peter the Great's "empress" daughters. Empress Elizabeth was renowned throughout Russia and beyond for her fierce commitment to the arts, particularly music and the lyric theater; Empress Anna fostered culture through theater and opera. And later, Catherine the Great entered the Russian cultural scene as a talented librettist, writer and aficionado of all forms of art. During the seventeenth and eighteenth centuries, each of Peter's daughters not only maintained private opera houses, but inspired hundreds of Italian composers to migrate to Russia to compose for the competing empresses.

Initially, Victor Hugo's *Ruy Blas* was suggested as the subject for the Russian commission, but Hugo's liberalism did not sit well with the court of Tsar Alexander II, whose censors rejected the work. Hugo's drama was essentially a thinly veiled cry for political reform during the reign of Spain's Charles II (1699). In the scenario, Ruy Blas, an indentured commoner and poet, dares to incept a love affair with the Queen.

The *Ruy Blas* play contained a contentious and vexing scenario, and after Verdi's recent conflicts with the censors for *Un Ballo in Maschera*, he was emotionally unprepared to enter into another battle. *Un Ballo*'s depiction of regicide was forbidden and Verdi was forced to substitute some of the opera's characterizations: its European royalty were transformed into petty rulers of the New World; and the opera's venue became colonial Boston, where Sweden's King Gustavus III became a colonial governor.

By mid-1861, Verdi became inspired to set the Spanish drama, *Don Álvaro o la fuerza del sino* (1835), ("Don Álvaro and the Force of Destiny") by Ángel de Saavedra, known as the 3rd Duke of Rivas (1791 – 1865).

Saavedra's *Don Álvaro* is generally considered a prototype and benchmark of the great flowering of Spanish romantic drama during the 1830s. It was joined by Antonio García Gutiérrez's *El Trovador* ("The Troubadour" — 1836); Juan Eugenio Hartzenbusch's *Los amantes de Teruel* ("The Lovers of Teruel" — 1837); and Martinez de la Rosa's *La Conjuración de Venezia* ("The Venetian Conspiracy of the year 1310" — 1834). Many of these dramatists had just returned from exile after having been earlier condemned for their liberal views.

In particular, Saavedra's *Don Álvaro* was a throbbing melodrama saturated with supercharged action; it was an archetype that many of the liberal Spanish dramatists were eager to follow — a true representation of the freedom of expression that Romanticism was obsessed to bring to the theater.

The play presented a narrative of the torrid passions of the mysterious Peruvian Don Álvaro and the acquiescent Donna Eleonora; it demonstrated how fate could intervene to bring about the destruction of Leonora's family at the hands of a man who loved her to distraction.

Victor Hugo's play *Hernani,* had established him as the father of French Romanticism, and heavily influenced Saavedra's *Don Álvaro.* In the spirit of Hugo's Romanticism, Saavedra dismissed all of the old Neoclassical rules: the drama's time-frame exceeded twenty-four hours; the action was set in two countries; prose alternated with verse; and the characters freely expressed their innermost feelings and intense passions.

Verdi's friend, Andrea Maffei, added an additional scene inspired by Friedrich Schiller's trilogy, *Wallensteins Lager,* indicating that Verdi was seeking to expand the scope of the opera scenario. In Schiller, Wallenstein rebels against Emperor Ferdinand II and is subsequently removed as commander-in-chief of the imperial army. But Verdi's primary interest was to capture Schiller's depiction of the panorama of life in a military encampment. In *La Forza,* Verdi adapted some of Schiller's spectacle scenes and incorporated sprawling action and picturesque scenes for his stage — like Schiller, Verdi often populated *La Forza*'s stage with soldiers, vivandieres, gypsies, astrologers, a preaching monk, et al.

The libretto was written by Francesco Maria Piave (librettist for the earlier *La Traviata* and *Rigoletto*) and bore the title *La Forza del Destino*, often translated as the *Power of Fate*, or *The Force of Destiny*.

Verdi left for Russia in 1861, but it became necessary to postpone the première owing to the illness of the prima donna. Nevertheless, during the subsequent year he took several trips to St. Petersburg to supervise rehearsals.

In November 1862, *La Forza del Destino* received moderate praise following its premiere at the Bolshoi Kamenny Theatre (Imperial Theatre) of St. Petersburg, Russia.

Audiences did not seem to object to the extremely powerful emotions and unbridled passions embedded in the original scenario of the opera, and at no point did reason become a factor in urging visceral restraint, since the horror of the plot twists were justified by the intervention of "fate" or "destiny." In Saavedra's original drama, all three of the main protagonists die: a wounded Carlo fatally stabs Leonora before he dies; and a shrieking Álvaro hurls himself over a precipice.

But after the St. Petersburg premiere of *La Forza*, a consensus arose that began to consider the plot excessively grim and foreboding, excessively lengthy, and horrific and terrifying. The opera's conclusion — with three gruesome deaths — suggested a deluge of blood filling Verdi's stage — seemingly a preview of the terrifying horror of the forthcoming French Grand Guignol genre of theater.

A chorus of dissatisfaction began to emerge from Piave as well as from critics. Piave wrote: "Our first problem is the finale. We've got to get rid of all those corpses."

But after Piave became paralyzed by a stroke, Verdi was forced to seek another librettist who would be capable of revising *La Forza*'s denouement. Verdi turned to Antonio Ghislanzoni, soon to become the librettist for *Aida.*

Verdi extensively re-worked the drama and essentially changed the tone of the entire work so that a well-defined balance of theatrical events became appropriate within the dramaturgy of the ultimate tragedy.

The "Ghislanzoni" revision added a final scene to Act III, a logical sequence following the duel between Carlo and Álvaro. Essentially, the ending was softened so that the body count of the final scene was reduced by one — the elimination of Álvaro's catastrophic suicide. In the new denouement, Álvaro renounces life and seeks redemption and religious consolation rather than suicide. However, the surviving Álvaro lives in despair, condemned to suffer from his memory of the fate of his beloved Leonora. Nevertheless, the concept of redemption provided the occasion for the stirring conclusion of the opera: "Non imprecarmi!"

The most significant "Ghislanzoni" revision was a new full-scale overture, which replaced the original brief prelude. In that sense, Verdi considered the work an "opera of ideas": therefore, the overriding dramatic concept of the opera, which is malevolent destiny, became the most significant leitmotif of the Overture — Leonora's fear and horror in being pursued by her avenging brother, Don Carlo.

However, the emphatic presence of the main theme (s) of the overture — the "destiny" or "fate" motifs — advance the idea of the score's "musical unity" — and the recurring elements provide a subtle continuity of musical ideas in the music score.

The "Ghislanzoni" revisions premiered at La Scala, Milan, in February 1869, seven years after the opera's St. Petersburg premiere, and ever since it has become the definitive performance version, an acclaimed masterpiece of the Italian lyric theater.

La Forza del Destino chronicles the chaotic events affecting Don Álvaro, a Peruvian of Incan descent, and the Spanish aristocrat, Leonora di Vargas; the lovers' romantic passions lead to Álvaro's fateful accidental murder of Leonora's father, the Marquis di Calatrava, which becomes the opera's singular dramatic impulse supporting Carlo's consuming passion for revenge, and his later retribution against his sister Leonora.

Saavedra's drama chronicles some of the history and intrigue of Álvaro and his family, in particular, the reason Álvaro was visiting Spain. Álvaro's father was a Viceroy of Peru, who had married the last descendant of the Inca monarchs. After his father's unsuccessful attempt to seize the throne and establish an independent kingdom, the Spanish government imprisoned him. Álvaro, the Viceroy's son, had come to Spain to plead for his father's release.

(The Inca Empire of Peru was the largest Spanish possession in South America. In 1542, Pizarro established the Viceroyalty of Peru with jurisdiction over most of Spanish-South America. Peru declared its independence from Spain in 1821, which ended the Viceroyalty. But during Spanish rule, Peru had become a principal source of Spanish wealth and power in South America, principally through silver mining.)

Primarily, Verdi's *La Forza* confronts the romantic theme of thwarted love. The Marquis became horrified when he discovered that Leonora planned to elope with Álvaro, a Peruvian Indian of Incan descent. No doubt, there was tension in the fact that Leonora and Álvaro emerged from a different class of society, and one can assume that the Marquis harbored the same prejudicial notions as those of the earlier Spanish "conquistadors," who considered many of their Indian victims to be inhuman savages. Nevertheless, the Marquis' underlying racial bias provided sufficient rationale for him to violently object to his daughter's romantic predilection.

After discovering the Incan Álvaro with Leonora, the Marquis unhesitatingly challenged Álvaro to a duel. But Álvaro refused to fight. Instead, he invoked a noble gesture in which he vowed to the Marquis that his daughter remained chaste — to further emphasize his convictions, he offered his life as a sacrifice to her honor.

Nevertheless, the Marquis became literally shocked upon finding the Incan Álvaro and Leonora together. He denounces Álvaro: "Vil seduttor!" ("Vile seducer!"), and then Leonora "Infame figlia!" ("Shameless daughter!") He is unhesitant in condemning Álvaro's roots: "No, la condotta vostra da troppo abbietta origine uscito vi dimostra" ("No, your conduct shows the baseness of your origins," and to Leonora before dying, "Lungi da me! Contamina tua vista la mia morte" ("Away from me! The sight of you stains my death!")

Álvaro surrenders by throwing his pistol to the floor. The inexplicable manifestation of fate intervenes and causes the pistol to fire when it strikes the floor, fatally wounding the Marquis. Leonora rushes to embraces her father, who curses his daughter just before dying: "Ti maledico." ("I curse you.")

Madness, delirium and chaos follow the incredible intervention of fate that dominates the events of the melodrama. But fate shares the mysterious manifestation of the Marquis' curse, as both powers drive the drama.

A curse invokes divine power to exact retribution through harm or misfortune. A curse — also referred to as a jinx, hex or execration — is any expressed wish in which adversity or misfortune shall befall or cling to some other entity — one or more persons, a place, or an object. In particular, a curse may refer to a wish that harm or hurt will be inflicted by any supernatural powers, such as a spell, a prayer, an imprecation, an execration, magic, witchcraft, God, a natural force, or a spirit. In many belief systems, the curse itself (or accompanying ritual) is considered to have some causative force. To reverse or eliminate a curse it must be removed or broken, a process often believed to require equally elaborate rituals or prayers.

Curses have a powerful dramatic effect: in Wagner's *The Ring of the Nibelung,* Alberich's curse on the Ring after the Gods seize it from him provides the dramatic — if not dynamic thread of the entire four music dramas. And the Verdi/Piave adaptation of Hugo's *Le Roi s'Amuse,* later titled *Rigoletto* (1851), was initially titled *La Maledizione* ("The Curse").

In *Rigoletto,* Monterone's curse on the jester becomes the central dramatic engine that haunts Rigoletto throughout the drama. It is initially a curse upon the licentious Duke for dishonoring Monterone's daughter — a rape by the debaucher for which Monterone invokes divine retribution. But after Rigoletto impudently mocks the old man's anguish and agony, the outraged Monterone curses both the Duke and Rigoletto and proceeds to vent his full rage on the audacious jester: "E tu, serpente, tu che d'un padre ridi al dolore, sii maledetto!" ("And you serpent, who mock a father's agony, be accursed!") Monterone's curse on a father demonizes and condemns the brazen Rigoletto, causing the jester to be overwhelmed by incomprehensible fear. For Rigoletto, the curse explains the tragic events that befall him: "Quel vecchio maledivami" ("That old man cursed me!")

The church always considered curses antithetical. For *Rigoletto*, the Austrian monarchy, a not-so-subtle theocracy uniting church and state, considered curse themes blasphemously offensive and an impropriety; censorship became their means to eliminate curses from the arts and the theater. Nevertheless, Verdi and Piave eventually brought the Hugo story to the opera stage without the censor's severe mutilation or alteration of the story's dramatic substance.

In Verdi's *La Forza*, the Marquis' curse of his daughter Leonora becomes monomaniacal, driving powerful vindictive forces that invoke divine retribution and exact harm or misfortune.

The Marquis had two sons, Don Carlo and Alfonso: the first was military officer; the second a student of law. Both became obsessed to pursue the guilty Álvaro and exact revenge. However, the accursed Leonora was deemed an accomplice in causing the tragedy the Marquis' murder and the curse demanded retribution as a necessary divine action that would denounce and purge her evil.

(In 1700, Charles II died, the last Hapsburg monarch to occupy the Spanish throne. A feverish struggle for control of the Spanish throne ensued, which resulted in the War of the Spanish Succession (1701— 1713). Spain's interests were largely subordinated to the dynastic and political intrigues of its only ally, Louis XIV, France's Bourbon king. Spain and France were opposed in the war by Leopold I, the Austrian Hapsburg Holy Roman Emperor and his allies, England, the Netherlands, and Prussia.)

In a strange materialization of fate, Álvaro and Carlo meet in Italy after both had enlisted in the War of the Spanish Succession. Carlo believes that fate brought him from Spain to Italy for the purpose of avenging his father's murder. At this juncture, he has become virtually insane from his obsession for revenge, not only against Álvaro, but also against his rebellious sister Leonora, the cause of the murder.

The opera progresses as a series of seemingly eternal chases and vain pursuits as each of the protagonists passes through different parts of Italy and Spain over a period of years. All three principal protagonists assume false identities that ironically unfold at their eventual and fatal reunion. Each protagonist is eventually involved in war, sword fights, false oaths, religious confessions, flights into mountain solitudes and church cloisters. They all live in a constant state of intense emotionalism and dreaded fear, and are constantly in conflict with themselves and all those surrounding them.

In the final act Verdi's musical inventions overflow with awesome wonder as the agitated theme of destiny underscores Leonora's appearance and her entreaties to God for peace: "Pace, pace, pace mio Dio!" — music of outstanding melodic sumptuousness and incandescence.

And the exquisite lyricism of the final music demonstrates Verdi's melodic genius as Father Guardiano castigates Father Raffaelo: "Non imprecare, umiliati a Lui che è giusto, che è giusto e santo" ("Do not curse. Humble yourself before Him who is just and holy!")

There exists a host of artistic creations that dwell on fate and curses, but few capture the intensely dramatic impact of the concept of uncontrollable and malevolent destinies as Verdi's *La Forza del Destino.*

Like "Fate" itself, the power of Verdi's score is undeniable. Cruel destiny separates father from daughter, brother from sister, and the intense romantic passions of the two young lovers. The melodrama includes the curse of a dying father, a blood feud, hate, sword fighting, and the all-consuming passions of revenge and retribution.

Verdi's magnificent musical inventions transform a rather perplexing and disquieting melodrama into one of the most compelling and turbulent works for the lyric theater; the opera is saturated with a rich abundance of melodic invention and colorful and mature harmonic development.

But love and betrayal dominate the interplay of passions of *La Forza del Destino*'s protagonists: all represent powerless humanity, victimized by the incomprehensible forces of "fate" and "destiny."

Principal Characters in La Forza del Destino

Marquis of Calatrava, Leonora's father	Bass
Leonora di Vargas, his daughter	Soprano
Don Carlos di Vargas, his son	Baritone
Don Álvaro, a Peruvian (Inca) nobleman	Tenor

Preziosilla, a gypsy (Mezzo-soprano); Padre Guardiano, (Father Superior), a Franciscan Friar (Bass); Fra Melitone, a Franciscan friar (Baritone); Curra, Leonora's maid (Mezzo-soprano); the Alcalde, or Mayor (Bass); Trabuco, a muleteer, later a peddler (Tenor); a Surgeon (Bass); Muleteers; Spanish and Italian peasants; Spanish and Italian soldiers; orderlies; Italian recruits; Franciscan Friars; poor mendicants; vivandieres; dancers; peasants; innkeeper; innkeeper's wife; servants at the Inn; drummers; buglers; peasants and children; a tumbler; peddlers

Time: 1701 —1713, during the Spanish War of Succession
Place: Spain and Italy

Brief Story Synopsis

Leonora di Vargas is about to elope with Don Álvaro, a Peruvian noble.

Leonora's father, the Marquis of Calatrava, opposes the union. Subsequently, the Marquis is accidentally killed by Álvaro.

Before dying, the Marquis curses Leonora. Don Carlos, Leonora's brother, vows to avenge his father's murder.

Leonora finds refuge from her avenging brother by living as a hermit.

Eventually, Álvaro becomes a friar and lives incognito as Father Raffaelo.

Carlos discovers Álvaro and insists on dueling with him.

They duel near the cave where Leonora has been secluded.
Carlos is mortally wounded. Álvaro seeks a friar to administer Carlos's last rites, and discovers Leonora.

Carlos dies, but not before stabbing Leonora to death.

Álvaro remans a friar, seeking redemption.

Overture to La Forza del Destino

In 1869, *Verdi* composed a new *Overture* for *La Forza del Destino,* which replaced the "preludio" of the original 1862 score.

The "Fate" chords ominously begin the *Overture:* six brass exclamations in unison. Each chord is played three times, which creates a somber atmosphere of "Fate" and foreboding — dark shadows that suggest doom and Leonora's tragic destiny.

The "Fate" theme is followed by an *Allegro agitato,* a provocative motif expressing fear and anxiety. The "Fate" theme is always associated with Leonora — she is its doomed victim; each time it occurs there is a sense of sinister fatality. It is particularly prominent when Leonora appears at the monastery of the Madonna degli Angeli, dressed in male clothes and about to pray for the Virgin's forgiveness: "Madre, pietosa Vergine" ("Mother, merciful Virgin, forgive my sin.") The theme also suggests the death of Leonora's father, the Marquis, and his subsequent curse of Leonora.

An *Andante* provides the melodic climax of Leonora's aria in Act II — Scene 2, "Madre pietosa vergine," in which she calls upon God for mercy — that He not abandon her to sorrow and misfortune. "Deh! Non m'abbandonar, pietà di me, Signore." ("In Thy mercy, O Lord, do not abandon me!")

An *Andantino* recalls the bitterness and hatred between Don Carlos and Don Álvaro. In the final act (Act IV), Álvaro pleads unsuccessfully with Carlos to resolve their enmity and invoke reason and understanding.

"Le minaccie, i fieri accenti, portin seco in preda i venti; perdonatemi, pietà, o fratel, pietà, pietà!" ("Fierce words and threats, be carried off by the wind. Forgive, have pity, have pity, brother, have pity, have pity.")

The *Allegro brillante* underscores Leonora's prayer for mercy, an exquisite cantilena that she pours out before entering the Monastery.

"Tua grazia, o Dio, sorride all rejetta" ("Eternal God, may Thy mercy shine on one who has been rejected.")

The musical expressiveness of the *Overture* is majestically designed.

"Destiny" remains the dominant theme of the *Overture:* it appears at the very beginning of the *Overture,* and at later moments of the opera, most often when Leonora expresses her inability to survive the consequences of "Fate."

Story Narrative with Music Highlight Examples

Act I: Seville, early eighteenth century. Leonora's room in the Marquis' home.

Leonora di Vargas is deeply in love with Don Álvaro, a Peruvian noble of Incan descent. However, she is conflicted: she is certain that her father will forbid her to marry a Peruvian of Incan blood, and has resolved that her only alternative is to elope with Álvaro.

Leonora bids goodnight to her father, the Marquis of Calatrava, and then sadly laments that her family will never accept her lover, Don Álvaro.

Me pellegrina ed orfana

A lighted candle from the balcony signals the arrival of Álvaro.

Álvaro and Leonora reunite, and express the ecstasy of their love for one another.

Ah, per sempre, or mio bell'angiol

Álvaro urges Leonora to hasten: steeds are waiting; a priest waits at the altar.

Ah! Seguirti fina agl'ultimi

Leonora begs Álvaro to wait one more day before they elope; she feels confident that she can secure her father's approval for their marriage.

But Álvaro assumes that Leonora's faltering determination signifies a change of emotions. Leonora then falls into Álvaro's arms and reassures him of her love, and further declaring that she is ready to flee with him.

Pronti destrieri

The Marquis and servants are awakened by noises emanating from the courtyard. After investigating them, he finds himself challenging Álvaro to a sword duel.

However, Álvaro is determined to avoid combat and hurls his sword and pistol to the floor. The pistol fires accidentally, fatally wounding the Marquis, who curses his daughter just before dying.

Afterwards, the lovers flee.

Act II - Scene 1: An inn at Hornachuelos.

After the accidental murder of the Marquis di Calatrava, Álvaro and Leonora fled, but in the confusion of being pursued, they were separated. Leonora desperately fears the enmity of her avenging brother, Carlos, who travels in disguise as he pursues Leonora and Álvaro.

Leonora turns to despair after having lost all trace of Álvaro. Her only salvation is to seek refuge in a Franciscan monastery, where she hopes to be admitted through the intercession of Father Cleto.

Amid peasants and muleteers, Leonora recognizes Carlos, but hides, unnoticed by her brother.

Crowds gather as soldiers are being recruited for a campaign in Italy.

A sprightly chorus hails the arriving muleteers.

Holà, holà, holà, ben giungi o mulattier

Preziosilla, a gypsy fortune-teller, introduces a rousing song that inspires the morale of the Italian and Spanish soldiers in their forthcoming battle against the Austrian Hapsburg armies.

Al suon del tamburo

While unnoticed, Leonora overhears Carlos reveal that Álvaro has fled abroad; she feels abandoned and betrayed.

Preziosilla reads Carlos's fortune and predicts a future of misfortune.

Pilgrims arrive, en route to Holy Week celebrations. All join in prayer, punctuated by Leonora's desperate cries for divine mercy.

Padre Eterno, Signor, pietà di noi

After the Pilgrims depart, Carlos delivers a narrative ballad to those pesent. He is masquerading as "Pereda," a medical student from Salamanca, and claims that he has been helping a friend track down a friend's sister and her lover, a biographical explication of his pursuit of his father's murderers.

Son Pereda, son ricco d'onore

Act II – Scene 2: Outside the church and monastery of the Madonna degli Angeli.

Leonora, dressed in male clothes, arrives at the Monastery degli Angeli. She recalls her despair after learning that Álvaro is alive, but that he has returned to Peru.

As evening prayers are heard from within the Monastery, Leonora falls to her knees, and begs for divine forgiveness and the Virgin's protection.

Madre, Madre, pietosa Vergine

Leonora sounds the monastery bell. She is greeted by the gruff Friar Melitone, who attempts to send her away until the next morning. But he changes his mind after she informs him that she has been sent by Father Cleto to meet with Padre Guardiano.

As Melitone seeks Father Guardiano, Leonora prays that God will not abandon her.

Deh! non m'abbandonar, pietà

With Padre Guardiano, Leonora relates her misfortunes: the accidental murder of her father, her brother's obsession for revenge, and her father's curse upon her. She is a rejected woman in need of the church in order to be redeemed.

Infelice, delusa rejetta

Guardiano agrees to help Leonora. He informs her of a deserted cave in the nearby mountains where she can live peacefully as a hermit: that anyone invading her seclusion shall be cursed.

No. Venite fidente alla croce

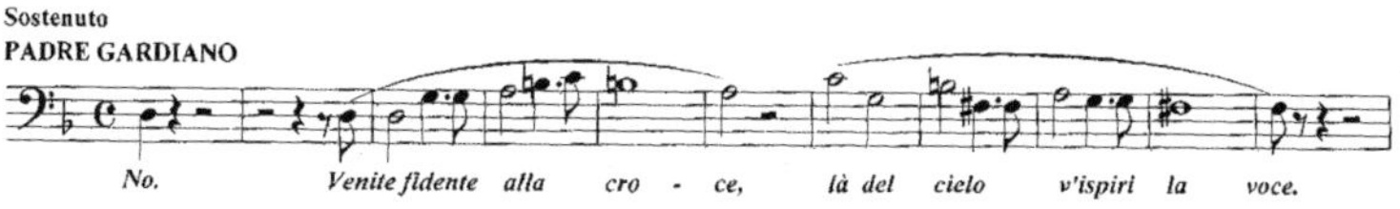

Father Guardiano has well understood Leonora's dilemma, and calls upon her to place her trust in God: to let the voice of Heaven speak to her heart. Leonora praises the peace of her forthcoming life.

Tua grazia, o Dio, sorride alla rejetta!

Calm overcomes Leonora as she reveals that her soul has finally found peace.

Più tranquilla l'alma sento

Guardiano provides Leonora with a Franciscan habit.

In an affecting prayer, Leonora, Guardiano and the Friars, pray to the Virgin for her protection.

Vergine degli angeli

Leonora kisses the hand of Padre Guardiano, and then advances toward the hermit's cave. As the Friars retreat into the church, Guardiano extends his arms in the direction where Leonora has disappeared, and blesses her.

Act III – Scene 1: The camp of Spanish and Italian troops near Velletri, Italy.

Unknown to one another, both Álvaro and Carlos have enlisted as soldiers in the Spanish War of Succession. Álvaro believed that Leonora died and enlisted under the name of Don Frederico Herreros; he was immediately promoted to captain after demonstrating great courage on the battlefield.

But Álvaro remains in despair: he has become tormented by memories of the past and bewails his fate and the harshness of destiny. In a moment of tender melancholy he recalls his noble birth and unhappy childhood; he believes that Leonora is dead and prays that she may look down upon him from heaven.

Oh, tu che inseno agli angeli

Álvaro's reveries are interrupted by cries of distress from a man set upon by a gang of thieves and assassins near the camp.

Álvaro hastens to the wounded man's aid and rescues him, unaware that the man is Don Carlos, his sworn enemy.

But neither man is aware of the other's identity: each travels under an assumed name; and neither one recognizes the other.

Afterwards, they become close friends and swear their loyalty to one another.

A renewed enemy attack causes both to rush off to battle. Álvaro is mortally wounded. Carlos tries to rally his new friend, promising him the Order of Calatrava; after hearing the name, Álvaro reacts violently.

Together, Álvaro and Carlos poignantly vow eternal friendship, in both life and death — a farewell that generates the most fervent and intense emotion.

Solenne in quest'ora

Álvaro entrusts his new friend Carlos to perform a last request. He gives him a key to a packet of private letters, which he must vow to burn if Álvaro should die. Carlos becomes overcome by pity, and vows to fulfill his friend's bidding. Álvaro rejoices, content that his solemn wish will be fulfilled.

Destiny cannot be thwarted. Although tempted, Carlos does not open the package but muses on the possibility that Álvaro might be the "cursed Indian" who killed his father and dishonored his sister.

Carlos recalls Álvaro's emotional reaction to the name of Calatrava, and begins to suspect that he may be Leonora's seducer. He searches among Álvaro's belongings and finds a portrait of Leonora, his sister. He is tempted to break open the packet.

Urna fatale del mio destino

The surgeon announces Álvaro's imminent recovery. Carlos exults. His mortal enemy's life has been saved — and now he will exact revenge against Álvaro for the murder of his father. The idea of fulfillng revenge causes Carlos to break into savage joy.

Ah! Egli è salva! oh gioia immenso

Act III — Scene 2: It is morning. The quarters of a senior officer of the Spanish army.

Álvaro has fully recovered from his wounds. Carlos informs him that he has learned his identity, and that he now seeks to avenge his father's murder by challenging him to a duel. Álvaro tries to pacify him by swearing his innocence and worthiness: that he yearns for peace between them, and refuses to take up arms against Leonora's brother.

Carlos informs him that Leonora remains alive. Álvaro celebrates the news.

No, d'un imeni il vincolo

Carlos is implacable and threatens to kill Leonora. Álvaro draws his sword, which antagonizes Carlos, who becomes enraged. Both swear mutual defiance and begin to duel. Finally, after guards separate them, Carlos is dragged off. In disgust, Álvaro breaks his sword in two. He repents for his anger and vows to seek peace in a cloister.

Preziosilla predicts the soldiers' fortunes; Trabucco peddles cheap merchandise and novelties; and Fra Melitone, now an army chaplain, delivers an extremely witty moral sermon in which he lectures the soldiers to reform their ungodly ways.

Finally, Preziosilla, drum-string tied around her neck, leads a marching chorus — "Rataplan" — a military-style march.

Rataplan

Act IV – Scene 1: Five years later. Inside the monastery of the Madonna degli Angeli.

Fra Melitone doles out soup to a band of beggars. Padre Guardiano cautions Melitone against being impatient with the poor, since they all praise Father Raffaelo (Don Álvaro), a man of singular compassion. Several years earlier, Raffaelo found refuge in Guardiano's holy order, unaware that Leonora was living close by.

Carlos has finally discovered Álvaro's whereabouts: that he travels incognito as Father Raffaelo. He remains implacable in his obsession to kill Álvaro and restore his family's honor.

Álvaro becomes surprised when he beholds Carlos, whom he thought dead. Álvaro pleads for peace and self-restraint between them.

Le minaccie, i fieri accenti

But Carlos remains intractable to Álvaro's pleas: that vengeance rests with God. The implacable Carlos curses him with venomous insults about his Peruvian Indian blood.

Carlos insists that they fight to the death, but Álvaro refuses, claiming that he is now a man of peace, and fighting is anathema to his soul. Nevertheless, after both express mutual defiance, Álvaro seizes the weapon and the men rush off to duel.

Act IV – Scene 2: The rocky terrain before Leonora's hermitage.

Leonora emerges from her cave. She is pale and worn, suffering from the weakening effects of penance and her yearning for ever-elusive peace.

Pace, pace, pace, pace, mio Dio

After hearing a commotion nearby, Leonora retreats into the cave. But suddenly she is summoned forth by Father Raffaelo (Álvaro) who announces that a man is mortally wounded and requests that the hermit give absolution to a dying man.

Leonora becomes shocked after she recognizes Álvaro. Once again, Álvaro cries out in agony: he has killed Carlos, and again Calatrava blood has stained his hands.

Leonora embraces Carlos, who strikes her with a moral blow.

Padre Guardiano tries to calm Álvaro's frustrated rage. He then blesses Leonora. As she dies in Álvaro's arms, she appeals to God for humility and compassion.

Non imprecare, umiliati a Lui

END of OPERA

Libretto

Act I: ***The Marquis of Calatrava, with a candle in his hand, bids goodnight to his daughter Leonora.***

MARCHESE:
Buona notte, mia figlia. Addio, diletta.
aperto ancora è quel veron.

MARQUIS: *(embracing Leonora)*
Goodnight, daughter; goodnight, my dear.
Is that balcony window still open?

LEONORA:
Oh, angoscia!

LEONORA:
(What anguish!)

MARCHESE:
Nulla dice il tuo amor?
Perchè si triste?

MARQUIS:
Have you no word of affection?
Why are you so sad?

LEONORA:
Padre, signor...

LEONORA:
Father, my Lord...

MARCHESE:
La pura aura de' campi
pace al tuo cor donava.
Fuggisti lo straniero di te indegno.
A me lascia la cura dell'avvenir;
nel padre tuo confida che t'ama tanto.

MARQUIS:
The pure air of the country
has brought peace to your heart.
That unworthy foreigner has fled.
Let me care for your future;
trust your father, who loves you!

LEONORA:
Ah, padre!

LEONORA:
Ah, father!

MARCHESE:
Ebben, che t'ange? Non pianger.

MARQUIS:
Well, what troubles you? Do not weep.

LEONORA:
Oh, rimorso!

LEONORA:
(I feel so guilty!)

MARCHESE:
Ti lascio.

MARQUIS:
I'll leave you.

LEONORA:
Ah, padre mio!

LEONORA: *(embracing her father)*
Ah, father!

MARCHESE:
Ti benedica il cielo. Addio.

MARQUIS:
Heaven bless you. Goodnight.

LEONORA:
Addio.

LEONORA:
Goodnight!

The Marquis kisses Leonora. He then takes the candle and goes into his room. Curra follows the Marquis. Leonora is left alone, in tears.

CURRA:
Temea restasse qui fino a domani.
Si riapre il veron. Tutto s'appronti, e andiamo.

CURRA:
I was afraid he'd stay here till tomorrow!
I'll open the window again.
Let's get everything ready, and then go.

Leonora takes a bag from the wardrobe, which has been filled with linens and clothes.

LEONORA:
E si amoroso padre, avverso fia tanto ai voti miei?
No, no, decidermi non so.

LEONORA:
How could such a loving father
be so opposed to my wishes?
No, no, I can't make up my mind.

CURRA:
Che dite?

CURRA:
What are you saying?

LEONORA:
Quegli accenti nel cor,
come pugnali scendevanmi. Se ancor
restava, appreso il ver gli avrei.

LEONORA:
Those words pierced my heart
like daggers. Had he stayed longer,
I would have confessed the truth.

CURRA:
Domani allor nel sangue suo saria Don Alvaro, od a Siviglia prigioniero, e forse al patibol poi!

CURRA:
Then tomorrow Don Alvaro would lie
in his own blood, a prisoner in Seville,
or perhaps awaiting the scaffold.

LEONORA:
Taci.

LEONORA:
Quiet!

CURRA:
E tutto questo perchè ei volle amar chi non l'amava.

CURRA:
And all this because he sought the love of someone who didn't love him.

LEONORA:
Io non amarlo?
Tu ben sai s'io l'ami.
Patria, famiglia, padre per lui non abbandono?
Ahi, troppo, troppo sventurata sono!

LEONORA:
I not love him? You know well I love him.
Am I not leaving for him? Am I not abandoning my country, my family, and my father for him?
Ah, my misfortunes are too great!

Me, pellegrina ed orfana,
lungi dal patrio nido.
Un fato inesorabile
sospinge a stranio lido;
colmo di triste immagini,
da' suoi rimorsi affranto.
È il cor di questa misera.

My inexorable fate,
as an orphan and wanderer,
drives me towards an alien shore,
far from my native soil;
filled with gloomy fancies,
the heart of this unhappy being
is broken by remorse.

Dannato a eterno pianto.
Ti lascio, ahimè, con lacrime,
dolce mia terra, addio;
ahimè, non avrà termine
per mi sì gran dolore!
Addio.

Condemned to endless weeping.
I leave you, alas, in tears,
sweet homeland! Farewell!
Alas! There will be no end
to such great sorrow!
Farewell.

CURRA:
M'aiuti, signorina, più presto andrem.

CURRA:
Help me, madam, so we get away more quickly.

LEONORA:
S'ei non venisse?
E tardi. Mezzanotte è suonata!
Ah no, più non verrà!

LEONORA:
And if he doesn't come?
It's late. It's past midnight.
Ah no, he will not come now!

CURRA:
Qual rumore? Calpestio di cavalli!

CURRA:
What's that noise? It's the clatter of horses' hooves!

LEONORA:
È desso!

LEONORA:
It is he!

CURRA:
Era impossibili ch'ei non venisse!

CURRA:
He would not have failed to come!

LEONORA:
O Dio!

LEONORA:
Heaven!

CURRA:
Brando al timore.

CURRA:
Away with fear!

Don Alvaro enters Leonora's room from the balcony. The lovers embrace.

ALVARO:
Ah, per sempre, o mio bell'angiol,
ne congiunge il cielo adesso!
L'universo in questo amplesso
io mi veggo giubilar.

ALVARO:
Forever, my beautiful angel,
heaven has united us forever!
In this embrace I see
the whole universe rejoicing.

LEONORA:
Don Alvaro!

LEONORA:
Don Alvaro!

ALVARO:
Ciel, che t'agita?

ALVARO:
Heavens! Why are you agitated?

LEONORA:
Presso è il giorno.

LEONORA:
It is almost daybreak.

ALVARO:
Da lung'ora
mille inciampi tua dimora
m'han vietato penetrar;
Ma d'amor si puro e santo
nulla opporsi può all'incanto,
e Dio stesso il nostro palpito
in letizia tramutò.
Quelle vesti dal verone getta.

ALVARO:
You have long prevented me
from entering your home;
but nothing can resist the spell
of a love so pure and holy.
And God himself has transformed
our anxiety into joy.
Throw those clothes
down from the balcony.

LEONORA:
Arresta.

LEONORA: *(to Curra)*
Stop!

ALVARO:
No, no.
Seguimi, lascia omai la tua prigione.

ALVARO:
No, no.
Follow me. Leave now for your prison.

LEONORA:
Ciel, risolvermi non so.

LEONORA:
Oh heaven! I cannot bring myself to it.

ALVARO:

ALVARO:

Pronti destrieri di già ne attendono,
un sarcerdote ne asspetta all'ara.
Vieni, d'amore in sen ripara
che Dio dal ciel benedirà!
E quando il sole, nume dell'India,
di mia regale stirpe signore,
il mondo innondi del suo splendore,
sposi, o diletta, ne troverà.

Below, swift steeds await us;
a priest waits at the altar.
Come, take shelter in the bosom of a love
that God will bless from heaven!
And when the sun, god of the Indies,
lord of my royal race,
bathes the earth in his splendor,
he will find us happily married.

LEONORA:
È tarda l'ora.

LEONORA:
The hour is late.

ALVARO:
Su, via, t'affretta.

ALVARO:
Come along, hurry!

LEONORA:
Ancor sospendi.

LEONORA: (*to Curra)*
Wait a moment!

ALVARO:
Eleonora!

ALVARO:
Eleonora!

LEONORA:
Diman.

LEONORA:
Tomorrow.

ALVARO:
Che parli?

ALVARO:
What are you saying?

LEONORA:
Te prego, aspetta.

LEONORA:
I beg you, wait.

ALVARO:
Diman!

ALVARO:
Tomorrow!

LEONORA:
Dimani si partirà.
anco una volta il padre mio,
povero padre, veder desio;
e tu contento, gli è ver, ne sei?

Sì, perché m'ami, nè opporti dei;
anch'io, tu il sai, t'amo io tanto!
Ne son felice, oh cielo, quanto!
Gonfio di gioia ho il cor! Restiamo!
Sì mio Alvaro, io t'amo, io t'amo!

LEONORA:
We will leave tomorrow.
I want to see my father
once more. My poor father,
you agree, don't you?

Yes, because you love me,
and you know how much I love you!
Heaven has brought us such happiness!
Your love swells in my heart! Rest!
Yes, Alvaro, I love you! I love you!

ALVARO:
Gonfio hai di gioia il core, e lagrimi!
Come un sepolcro tua man è gelida!
Tutto comprendo, tutto, signora!

ALVARO:
Your heart is filled with joy, yet you weep!
Your hand is as cold as the tomb!
I understand everything now, my lady!

LEONORA:
Alvaro! Alvaro!

LEONORA:
Alvaro! Alvaro!

ALVARO:
Eleonora!
Io sol saprò soffrire. Tolga Iddio
che i passi miei per debolezza segua.

ALVARO:
Eleonora!
I shall learn to suffer alone. God forbid
that you follow me through weakness.

Sciolgo i tuoi giuri. Le nuziali tede
sarebbero per noi segnal di morte
se tu, com'io, non m'ami, se pentita.

I release you from your oath. To marry
would mean death for us, if you do not
love me as I love you, you will have regrets.

LEONORA:
Son tua, son tua col core e colla vita!
Seguirti, fino agli ultimi
confini della terra;
con te sfidar, impavida
di rio destin, la guerra,
mi fia perenne gaudio
d'eterea voluttà.
Ti seguo. Andiam,
Dividerci il fato non potrà.

LEONORA:
I am yours, with my heart and soul!
I will follow you to the furthest ends
of the earth;
I will fearlessly defy
the assault of evil fate.
Let these prizes endow me
with endless joy,
and heavenly delight!
Let us go because fate cannot keep us apart.

ALVARO:
Sospiro, luce ed anima
di questo cor che t'ama.
Finchè mi batte un palpito
far paga ogni tua brama
il solo ed immutabile
desio per me sarà.
Mi segui. Andiam.
Dividerci il fato non potrà.

ALVARO:
I breathe again, light and soul.
It is this heart that loves you;
so long as a breath of life is in me,
my sole, and my unchanging desire
shall be to fulfill
your every desire.
Follow me. Let's go.
Fate cannot keep us apart.

Sounds reveal that a door is being opened.

LEONORA:
Qual rumor!

LEONORA:
What is that noise?

CURRA:
Ascendono le scale!

CURRA:
They're coming up the stairs!

ALVARO e LEONORA:
Partiam!
Mi segui! Ti seguo. Andiam.
Dividerci il fato non potrà.

ALVARO and LEONORA:
Let's leave!
I'll follow you. Let's go.
No, fate cannot keep us apart.

LEONORA:
È tardi.

LEONORA:
It's too late!

ALVARO:
Allor di calma è duopo.

ALVARO:
Then we must keep calm.

CURRA:
Vergin santa!

CURRA:
Holy Virgin!

LEONORA:
Colà t'ascondi.

LEONORA: *(to Don Alvaro)*
Hide in there.

ALVARO:
No. Difenderti degg'io.

ALVARO: *(drawing a pistol)*
No, I must protect you.

LEONORA:
Ripon quell'arma. Contro al genitore vorresti?

LEONORA:
Put away that gun.
Would you raise it against my father?

ALVARO:
No, contro me stesso!

ALVARO:
No, against myself!

LEONORA:
Orrore!

LEONORA:
Horror!

The door opens. The Marquis of Calatrava appears. He is furious. He brandishes his sword. Two servants follow him, carrying lamps.

MARCHESE:
Vil seduttor! Infame figlia!

MARQUIS:
Vile seducer! Shameless daughter!

LEONORA:
No, padre mio.

LEONORA: *(throwing herself at his feet)*
No, father.

MARCHESE:
Io più nol sono.

MARQUIS: *(repulsing her)*
I am no longer your father!

ALVARO:
Il solo colpevole son io.
Ferite, vendicatevi.

ALVARO: *(to the Marquis)*
I alone am the guilty one.
Strike at me - take your revenge!

MARCHESE:
No, la condotta vostra da troppo abbietta origine.

MARQUIS: *(to Alvaro)*
No, your conduct shows the baseness of your origins.

ALVARO:
Signor Marchese!

ALVARO:
My lord!

MARCHESE:
Scostati.
S'arresti l'empio.

MARQUIS:
Stand aside.
Arrest the scoundrel!

ALVARO:
Guai se alcun di voi si muove.

ALVARO: *(takes out the pistol again)*
Beware, if either of you moves.

LEONORA:
Alvaro, oh ciel, che fai?

LEONORA: *(running to Alvaro)*
Alvaro - heavens, what are you doing?

ALVARO:
Cedo a voi sol, ferite.

ALVARO: *(to the Marquis)*
I yield to you alone. Strike me!

MARCHESE:
Morir per mano mia! Per mano del carnefice
tal vita spenta sia!

MARQUIS:
Die by my hand! Let your life
be ended by the executioner!

ALVARO:
Signor di Calatrava!
Pura siccome gli angeli
è vostra figlia, il giuro;
reo sono io solo. Il dubbio
che l'ardir mio qui desta.
Sì tolga colla vita. Eccomi inerme.

ALVARO:
My Lord of Calatrava!
Your daughter is as pure as the angels
- I swear it;
I alone am guilty. Let the suspicion
aroused by my boldness be removed.
Here I stand, unarmed.

Alvaro throws his pistol to the ground. After it strikes the ground it accidentally fires, mortally wounding the Marquis.

MARCHESE:
Io muoio!

MARQUIS:
I am dying!

ALVARO:
Arma funesta!

ALVARO: *(desperately)*
Fatal weapon!

LEONORA:]
Aita!

LEONORA: *(running to her father's side)*
Help!

MARCHESE:
Lungi da me.
Contamina tua vista la mia morte!

MARQUIS: *(to Leonora)*
Get away from me! The sight of you taints
my death!

LEONORA:
Padre!

LEONORA:
Father!

MARCHESE:
Ti maledico!

MARQUIS:
I curse you!

The mortally wounded Marquis falls into the arms of his servants.

LEONORA:
Cielo, pietade!

ALVARO: *(in desperation)*
Heaven, have mercy!

ALVARO:
Oh, sorte!

ALVARO:
Oh, what a cruel destiny!

Servants carry the Marquis to his apartments.
Don Alvaro drags the grieving Leonora with him as they exit.

END of Act I

Act II: — Scene 1:
An Inn in the village of Hornachuelos. The innkeeper and his wife are busy preparing supper. The Alcalde sits near the fire; a student (Don Carlos in disguise) sits near him. Muleteers, among them Trabuco sits in front. Two pairs of villagers, the serving-wench and a muleteer dance a seguidilla.

CORO:

CHORUS:

Holà, holà, holà!
Ben giungi, o mulattier,
La notte a riposar.
Holà, holà, holà!
Qui devi col bicchier
le forze ritemprar.

Holà, holà, holà!
Muleteers, you've done well
by coming here to rest for the night.
Holà, holà, holà!
Here you must renew your
strength with a glass!

The hostess sets a large tureen on the table.

ALCADE:
La cena è pronta.

ALCADE:
Supper's ready.

CORO:
A cena, a cena.

CHORUS: *(seating themselves)*
Let's eat.

CARLO:
Ricero invan la suora e il seduttore.
Perfidi!

CARLOS: *(disguised as a student)*
(In vain I seek my sister and her seducer.
Those dishonorable wretches!)

CORO:
Voi la mensa benedite.

CHORUS: *(to the Alcalde)*
You say Grace.

ALCADE:
Può farlo il licenziato.

ALCADE:
The learned scholar can say it.

CARLO
Di buon grado.
In nomine Patris, et Filii, et Spiritus Sancti.

CARLOS:
Willingly.
In nomine Patris, et Filii, et Spiritus Sancti.

CORO:
Amen.

CHORUS: *(seating themselves)*
Amen.

Leonora appears, dressed in men's clothing.

LEONORA:
(Che vedo! Mio fratello!)

LEONORA:
(What do I see! My brother!)

ALCADE:
Buono.

ALCALDE: *(tasting the food)*
It's good.

CARLOS:
Eccellente. Par che dica, "Mangiami"
Tu das epulis accumbere Divum.

CARLOS:
Excellent. It just asks to be eaten.
Tu das epulis accumbere Divam.

ALCADE:
Non sa il Latino, ma cucina bene.

ALCALDE:
She knows no Latin, but she cooks well.

CARLOS:
Viva l'ostessa!

CARLOS:
Three cheers for the hostess!

TUTTI:
Evviva!

ALL:
Hurrah!

CARLOS:
Non vien, Maestro Trabuco?

CARLOS:
Aren't you coming, Master Trabuco?

TRABUCO:
È venerdì.

TRABUCO:
It's Friday!

CARLOS:
Digiuna?

CARLOS:
Are you fasting?

TRABUCO:
Appunto.

TRABUCO:
That's right.

CARLOS:
E qella personcina con lei giunta?

CARLOS:
And that little person who came with you?

PREZIOSILLA:
Viva la guerra!

PREZIOSILLA:
Hurrah for the war!

TUTTI:
Preziosilla! Brava, brava! Qui, presso a me!

ALL:
Preziosilla! Brava! Here, sit next to me.

CARLOS:
Tu la ventura dirne potrai.

CARLOS:
Can you tell our fortunes.

PREZIOSILLA:
Chi brama far fortuna?

PREZIOSILLA:
Who wants to know his fortune?

TUTTI:
Tutti il vogliamo.

ALL:
We all do!

PREZIOSILLA:
Correte allor soldati in Italia, dov'è rotta la guerra contro il Tedesco.

PREZIOSILLA:
Then go as soldiers to Italy, where war has broken out against the Germans.

TUTTI:
Morte ai Tedeschi!

ALL:
Death to the Germans!

PREZIOSILLA:
Flagel d'Italia eterno, e de figlioli suoi.

PREZIOSILLA:
The eternal scourge of Italy and her sons.

TUTTI:
Tutti v'andremo.

ALL:
Let's all go.

PREZIOSILLA:
Ed io sarò con voi.

PREZIOSILLA:
And I am with you.

TUTTI:
Viva!

ALL:
Hurrah!

PREZIOSILLA:

PREZIOSILLA:

Al suon del tamburo,
Al brio del corsiero,
Al nugolo azzurro
Del bronzo guerrier;
Dei campi al sussurro
S'esalta il pensiero!
È bella la guerra, è bella la guerra!
Evviva la guerra, evviva!

At the sound of the drum,
at the mettle of the steed,
at the blue cloud
of the cannon of war.
At the bustle of the camp,
the spirits rise.
War is splendid!
Hurrah for war!

È solo obliato
da vile chi muore;
al bravo soldato,
al vero valor
è premio serbato
di gloria, d'onor!

He who dies a coward,
he alone is forgotten;
he who dies a coward,
is not the brave soldier;
true valor is the reward
of glory and honor.

Se vieni, fratello,
sarai caporale;
e tu colonnello,
e tu generale.

How splendid war is!
Hurrah for war!
If you come, brother, you'll be a corporal,
and you a colonel, and you a general.

Il dio furfantello
dall'arco immortale
farà di cappello
al bravo uffiziale.
È bella la guerra, evviva la guerra!

The little roguish god
of the immortal bow
will salute the brave officer.
How splendid is war!
Hurrah for war!

TUTTI:
È bella la guerra, evviva la guerra!

CHORUS:
Hurrah for war!

CARLOS:
E che riserbasi allo studente?

CARLOS: *(showing his palm)*
And what's in store for the student?

PREZIOSILLA:
Ah, tu miserrime vicende avrai.

PREZIOSILLA: *(reading at his hand)*
You will have most wretched experiences.

CARLOS:
Che di'?

CARLOS:
What are you saying?

PREZIOSILLA:
Non mente il labbro mai.
Ma a te, carissimo,
non presto fè.

PREZIOSILLA: *(gazing at him)*
My lips never lie.
But, my dear lad,
your fate is near.

Non sei studente,
non dirò niente,
ma, gnaffe, a me
non se la fa,
tra la la la!

You're not a student,
and I'll say nothing,
but no one takes me in.-
no, upon my word,
tra la la la!

A band of pilgrims are heard praying in the distance.

CORO DI PELLEGRINI:

CHORUS OF PILGRIMS:

Padre Eterno Signor,
Pietà di noi,
Divin Figlio Signor,

Eternal Father, Lord,
have mercy on us.
Divine Son, Lord,

Pietà di noi.
Santo Spirito Signor,
Pietà di noi.
Uno e Trino Signor,
Pietà di noi.

have mercy on us.
Sainted Spirit, Lord,
have mercy upon us.
Holy Trinity, Lord,
have mercy on us.

TUTTI:
Chi sono?

CHORUS:
Who are they?

ALCADE:
Son pellegrini che vanno al giubileo.

ALCALDE:
Pilgrims on their way to the celebration.

LEONORA:
Fuggir potessi!

LEONORA: *(with great agitation)*
(If only I could escape!)

TUTTI:
Che passino attendiamo.

ALL:
Let's wait till they've gone by.

ALCADE:
Preghiam con lor.

ALCALDE:
Let us pray with them.

TUTTI:
Preghiamo.
Su noi prostrati e supplici
stendi la man, Signore;
dall'infernal malore
ne salvi tua bontà.
Signor, pietà!

ALL:
Let us pray.
Prostrate and supplicant,
extend Thy hand over us, O Lord;
may Thy goodness save us
from infernal perdition.
O Lord, have mercy!

LEONORA:
Ah, dal fratello salvami
che anela il sangue mio;
se tu nol vuoi, gran Dio,
nessun mi salverà!
Signor, pietà!

LEONORA: *(to herself)*
(Ah, save me from a brother
who thirsts for my blood.
If Thou wilt not, great God,
no one will save me!
O Lord, have mercy!)

CARLOS:
Viva la buona compagnia!

CARLOS:
Here's to our good company!

TUTTI:
Viva!

ALL:
Hurrah!

CARLOS:
Salute qui, l'eterna gloria poi.

CARLOS: *(lifting his glass)*
To health here, eternal glory later!

TUTTI:
Così sia.

ALL:
Hear, hear!

CARLOS:
Già cogli angeli, Trabuco?

CARLOS:
Are you ready for the angels, Trabuco?

TRABUCO:
E che? Con quest'inferno!

TRABUCO:
What? In this hell-hole?

CARLOS:
E quella personcina con lei giunta,
venne pel giubileo?

CARLOS:
And did that little person with you
come for the celebration?

TRABUCO:
Nol so.

TRABUCO:
I don't know.

CARLOS:
Per altro, è gallo oppur gallina?

CARLOS:
By the way - is it a cock or a hen?

TRABUCO:
De' viaggiator non bado che al danaro.

TRABUCO:
A traveler's money is all I notice.

Molto prudente!

Very prudent of you.
(turning to the Alcalde)

Ed ella che giungere la vide,
perchè a cena non vien?

You saw him arrive.
Why didn't he come to supper?

ALCADE:
L'ignoro.

ALCADE:
I don't know.

CARLOS:
Dissero chiedesse acqua ed aceto. Ah, ah!
Per rinfrescarsi.

CARLOS:
It's said he asked for vinegar and water.
Ha, ha! To refresh himself.

ALCADE:
Sarà.

ALCADE:
It may be so.

CARLOS:
È ver che è gentile e senza barba?

TRABUCO:
It's true that he's delicate and beardless?

ALCADE:
Non so nulla.

ALCADE:
I know nothing.

CARLOS:
Parlar non vuol!

CARLOS: *(to himself)*
(He won't talk.)

Ancora lei:
Stava sul mulo
Seduta o a cavalcioni?

(to Trabuco)
I turn to you again.
Did he ride the mule
side-saddle or astride?

TRABUCO:
Che noia!

TRABUCO: *(impatiently)*
This is a bore!

CARLOS:
Onde veniva?

CARLOS:
Where did he come from?

TRABUCO:
So che andrò presto o tardi in Paradiso.

TRABUCO:
I know sooner or later I'll go to heaven!

CARLOS:
Perchè?

CARLOS:
Why?

TRABUCO:
Ella il Purgatorio mi fa soffrire.

TRABUCO:
Because you're making me suffer purgatory.

CARLOS:
Or dove va?

CARLOS:
Where are you going now?

TRABUCO:
In istalla a dormir colle mie mule, che non san di latino, nè sono baccellieri.

TRABUCO:
To the stable, to sleep with my mules, who know no Latin and aren't Bachelors of Arts.

Carlos takes his saddle and departs.

TUTTI:
Ah, ah! È fuggito!

ALL:
Ha, ha - he's fled!

CARLOS:
Poich' è imberbe l'incognito,
facciamgli col nero due
baffetti; doman ne rideremo.

CARLOS:
Since the stranger is beardless, let's paint
him a moustache with lamp-black.
Tomorrow we'll have a good laugh at it.

TUTTI:
Bravo! Bravo!

ALL:
Bravo! Bravo!

ALCADE:
Protegger debbo i viaggiator; m'oppongo.
Meglio farebbe dirne d'onde venga, ove
vada, e chi ella sia.

ALCALDE:
I have to protect all travellers; I'm against
this. It would be better if you told us
where you're from, going, and who you are.

CARLOS:
Lo vuoi saper? Ecco l'istoria mia.

CARLOS:
Do you want to know? Here's my story.

Son Pereda, son ricco d'onore,
Baccelliere mi fe' Salamanca;
sarò presto in utroque dottore,
che di studio ancor poco mi manca.

I am Pereda, rich in honors;
Salamanca made me a Bachelor;
soon I shall be a full-fledged Doctor,
for I've only a few studies to complete.

Di là Vargas mi tolse da un anno,
ed a Siviglia con sè mi guidò.
Non tratenne Pereda alcun danno,
per l'amico il suo core parlò.

Vargas took me from there a year ago
and brought me with him to Seville.
Pereda would brook no affront;
his heart spoke out for his friend.

Della suora un amante straniero
colà il padre gli avea trucidato,
ed il figlio, da pro' cavaliero,
la vendetta ne aveva giurato.

A foreigner, his sister's lover,
had murdered his father there,
and the son, like the brave knight he is,
had sworn revenge.

Gl'inseguimmo di Cadice in riva,
nè la coppia fatal si trovò.
Per l'amico Pereda soffriva,
che il suo core per esso parlò.

We followed them to the coast at Cadiz,
but could not find the guilty pair.
Pereda suffered for his friend,
and his heart spoke out for him.

Là e dovunque narrar che del pari
La sedotta col vecchio peria,
che a una zuffa tra servi a sicari
Solo il vil seduttore sfuggìa.

There and everywhere alike, it was said
that the seduced girl had perished with her
father; in a scuffle between servants and
assassins, only the vile seducer escaped.

Io da Vargas allor mi staccava,
ei seguir l'assassino giurò.
Verso America il mare solcava,
e Pereda ai suoi studi tornò!

Then I separated from Vargas,
who swore to pursue the murderer.
He set sail for America,
and Pereda returned to his studies.

TUTTI:
Truce storia Pereda narrava!
Generoso il suo core mostrò.

ALL:
Pereda has told a grim story,
and shown his generosity of heart!

ALCADE:
Sta bene.

ALCALDE:
Very well.

PREZIOSILLA:
Ucciso fu quel Marchese?

PREZIOSILLA:
This Marquis was killed?

CARLO:
Ebben?

CARLOS:
Well?

PREZIOSILLA
L'assassino rapia sua figlia?

PREZIOSILLA:
And the assassin ravished his daughter?

CARLOS:
Sì.

CARLOS:
Yes.

PREZIOSILLA:
E voi, l'amico fido, cortese,
andaste a Cadice e pria a Siviglia?
Ah, gnaffe, a me non se la fa, tra la la la!

PREZIOSILLA:
And you, the faithful, noble friend, went
to Cadiz, and before that to Seville? No one
takes me in, no, 'pon my word, tra, la, la la!

ALCADE:
Figliuoli, è tardi; poichè abbiam cenato,
si rendan grazie a Dio, e partiamo.

ALCADE:
My sons, it's late; let us give thanks
to God for our meal, and then be off.

PREZIOSILLA, CARLOS e CORO
Partiam, partiam, partiamo. Buono notte.

PREZIOSILLA, CARLOS and CHORUS:
Let's be off. Good evening to all!

TUTTI:
Holà! Holà! È l'ora di riposar.
Allegri, o mulattier! Holà!

ALL:
Holà, holà! It's time to rest.
Look lively, muleteers!

PREZIOSILLA:
Ah, tra la la la!
Ma, gnaffe, a me no se la fa.

PREZIOSILLA:
Ha ha, tra la la la;
No one takes me in, 'upon my word!

TUTTI:
Buon notte. Andiam, andiam.

ALL:
Good night.

Act II — Scene 2: ***On the slope of a steep mountain stands the church of Our Lady of the Angels. Beyond the church, there are high mountains and the village of Hornachuelos. Leonora appears, exhausted from the climb. She is dressed in man's clothing, and wears a wide-sleeved cloak, broad-brimmed hat and riding boots.***

LEONORA:
Sono giunta! Grazie, o Dio!
Estremo asil guesto è per me!
Son giunta! Io tremo! La mia orrenda storia
è nota in quell'albergo, e mio fratel narrolla!

Se scoperta m'avesse! Cielo! Ei disse
naviga vers' occaso. Don Alvaro! Nè morto
cadde quella notte in cui io, io del sangue di
mio padre intrisa, l'ho seguito e il perde!
Ed or mi lascia, mi fugge!
Ohimè, non reggo a tanta ambascia.

LEONORA:
I'm here at last! Thanks be to Thee, O God!
This is my last refuge! I am here! I am
trembling! My dreadful story is known at
the inn - my own brother was telling it!

If he had discovered me! Heavens! He said
that Don Alvaro was sailing to the West!
He did not fall dead that night when I,
soaked in my father's blood, followed him,
but lost him! And now he leaves me, he
flees from me! Ah, I cannot bear such anguish!

Madre, pietosa Vergine,
perdona al mio peccato,
M'aita quel ingrato
dal core a cancellar.

Mother, merciful Virgin,
forgive my sin.
Help me to erase that ingrate
from my heart.

In queste solitudini
espierò l'errore,
Pietà di me, Signore.
Deh, non m'abbandonar!

In this seclusion
I will expiate my guilt.
Have mercy on me, Lord;
do not forsake me!

An organ accompanies the monks in their morning prayers.

CORO DEI FRATI:
Venite, adoremus et procedamus ante Deum,
Ploremus, ploremus coram Donino, coram Domino qui fecit nos.

CHORUS OF MONKS: *(in the church)*
Venite, adoremus et procedamus ante Deum.
Ploremus coram Domino, coram Domino, qui fecit nos.

LEONORA:
Al santo asilo accorrasi.
E l'oserò a quest'ora?
Alcun potria sorprendermi!
O misera Leonora, tremi?

LEONORA:
Ah, those sublime hymns and organ
harmonies rising like incense
to God in Heaven, inspire my soul
with faith, comfort and peace!

Il pio frate accoglierti no, non ricuserà.
Non mi lasciar, soccorrimi,
pietà Signor, pietà!
Deh, non m'abbandonar!

Do not forsake me, help me,
have mercy, Lord!
Do not abandon me, O Lord;
have mercy on me!

FRATI:
Ploremus, coram Donino qui fecti nos.

CHORUS OF MONKS:
Ploremus coram Domino, qui fecit nos.

Leonora rings the monastery bell. A window opens.
A lantern lights up Leonora's face. Fra Melitone speaks to her from within.

FRA MELITONE:
Chi siete?

MELITONE:
Who are you!

LEONORA:
Chiedo il Superiore.

LEONORA:
I wish to speak to the Superior.

FRA MELITONE:
S'apre alle cinque la chiesa,
Se al giubileo venite.

MELITONE:
The church opens at five o'clock,
if you have come for the celebration.

LEONORA:
Il Superiore, per carità,

LEONORA:
The Superior, for mercy's sake!

FRA MELITONE:
Che carità a quest'ora!

MELITONE:
What, charity at this hour?

LEONORA:
Mi manda il Padre Cleto.

LEONORA:
Father Cleto sent me.

FRA MELITONE:
Quel santo uomo? Il motivo?

MELITONE:
That saintly man? For what reason?

LEONORA:
Urgente.

LEONORA:
An urgent one.

FRA MELITONE:
Perché mai?

MELITONE:
What is it?

LEONORA:
Un infelice.....

LEONORA:
An unfortunate soul...

FRA MELITONE:
Brutta solfa, però v'apro ond'entriate.

MELITONE:
How sad! I'll open it for you to come in.

LEONORA:
Nol posso.

LEONORA:
I cannot.

FRA MELITONE:
No? Scomunicato siete? Che strano fia aspettare a ciel sereno. V'annuncio, e se non torno, buona notte.

MELITONE:
No? Are you excommunicated? How strange to wait out here! I'll announce you. If I don't come back, then goodnight.

LEONORA:
Ah, s'ei mi respingesse! Fama pietoso il dice; ei mi proteggerà. Vergin m'assisti.

LEONORA:
What if I'm rejected! It is said he is merciful. He will protect me. Holy Virgin, help me.

The Father Superior, Padre Guardiano, and Fra Melitone appear at the door.

PADRE GUARDIANO:
Chi mi cerca?

FATHER GUARDIANO:
Who asks for me?

LEONORA:
Son io.

LEONORA:
I do..

PADRE GUARDIANO:
Dite.

FATHER GUARDIANO:
Speak.

LEONORA:
Un segreto.

LEONORA:
It is a secret.

PADRE GUARDIANO:
Andate, Melitone.

FATHER GUARDIANO:
Let us go, Melitone.

FRA MELITONE:
Sempre segreti! E questi santi soli han da saperli!
Noi siamo tanti cavoli.

MELITONE:
(Always secrets!
And only these holy men must know them!
We're a bunch of cabbages!)

PADRE GUARDIANO:
Fratello, mormorate?

FATHER GUARDIANO:
Brother, What are you muttering?

FRA MELITONE:
Oibò, dico ch'è pesante la porta e fa rumore.

MELITONE:
Oh, I was saying that the door is heavy and makes noise.

PADRE GUARDIANO:
Obbedite.

FATHER GUARDIANO:
Obey me!

FRA MELITONE:
Che tuon da Superiore!

MELITONE:
(He's asserting his authority!)

PADRE GUARDIANO:
Or siam soli.

FATHER GUARDIANO:
Now we are alone.

LEONORA:
Una donna son io.

LEONORA:
I am a woman.

PADRE GUARDIANO:
Una donna a quest'ora! Gran Dio!

FATHER GUARDIANO:
A woman at this hour! Good Lord!

LEONORA:

LEONORA:

Infelice, delusa, rejetta,
dalla terra e del ciel maledetta,
che nel pianto protratavi al piede,
di sottrala all'inferno vi chiede.

One unhappy, deceived, rejected,
and accursed by both earth and heaven;
one who throws herself in tears at your feet
and begs you to rescue her from hell.

PADRE GUARDIANO:
Come un povero frate lo può?

FATHER GUARDIANO:
How can a poor monk do that?

LEONORA:
Padre Cleto un suo foglio v'inviò?

LEONORA:
Did Father Cleto not send you a note?

PADRE GUARDIANO:
Ei vi manda?

FATHER GUARDIANO:
He sent you?

LEONORA:
Sì.

LEONORA:
Yes.

FATHER GUARDIANO:
Dunque voi siete Leonora di Vargas!

FATHER GUARDIANO:
Then you are Leonora de Vargas!

LEONORA
Fremete!

LEONORA:
You shudder!

PADRE GUARDIANO:

FATHER GUARDIANO:

No, venite fidente alla croce,
Là del cielo v'ispiri la voce.

No. Come, trusting, to the Cross.
There may the voice of heaven inspire you.

LEONORA:

LEONORA:

Più tranquilla, l'alma sento
dacchè premo questa terra;
de' fantasmi lo spavento
più non provo farmi guerra.

I feel my soul calmer
since I trod this ground.
I no longer feel the terror
of phantoms assailing me.

Più non sorge sanguinante
di mio padre l'ombre innante,
nè terribile l'ascolto
la sua figlia maledir.

No longer does my father's ghost
rise, bleeding before me.
Nor do I hear him
fearully curse his daughter.

PADRE GUARDIANO:
Sempre indarno qui rivolto fu di Satana l'ardir.

FATHER GUARDIANO:
Satan's presumption has always been powerless here.

LEONORA:
Perciò tomba qui desio fra le rupi ov'altra visse.

LEONORA:
That is why I seek my tomb here among the rocks, where another woman lived.

PADRE GUARDIANO:
Che! Sapete?

FATHER GUARDIANO:
What! You know of her?

LEONORA:
Cleto il disse.

LEONORA:
Cleto told me.

PADRE GUARDIANO:
E volete?

FATHER GUARDIANO:
And you wish?

LEONORA:
Darmi a Dio.

LEONORA:
To give myself to God.

PADRE GUARDIANO:
Guai per chi si lascia illudere
dal delirio d'un momento!
Più fatal per voi si giovane
giungerebbe il pentimento.

Guai per chi si lascia illudere. Guai!
Chi può leggere il futuro? Chi immutabil
farvi il core? E l'amante?

FATHER GUARDIANO:
Woe to him who lets himself be misled
by the delirium of a moment!
Regret would prove fatal for one as young
as you are.

Woe to him who lets himself be misled.
Who can read into the future? Who can tell
your heart won't change? And your lover?

LEONORA:
Involontario m'uccise il genitor.

LEONORA:
He killed my father by accident.

PADRE GUARDIANO:
E il fratello?

FATHER GUARDIANO:
And your brother?

LEONORA:
La mia morte di sua mano egli giurò.

LEONORA:
He has sworn that I shall die by his hand.

PADRE GUARDIANO:
Meglio a voi le sante porte schiuda un
chiostro.

FATHER GUARDIANO:
Better that a convent should open its holy
doors to you.

LEONORA:
Un chiostro? No!
Se voi sacciate questa pentita
andrò per balze, girdando aita,
ricovro ai monti, cibo alle selve.

E fin le belve ne avran pietà.
Ah, sì, del cielo qui udii la voce:
"Salvati all'ombra di questa croce."
Voi mi scacciate? È questo il porto.
chi tal conforto mi toglierà?

LEONORA:
A convent? No.
If you drive this penitent away I shall beg
the mountains for refuge,
and the forest for food.

Here I have heard the voice of heaven:
"Take refuge in the shadow of this Cross."
And don't drive me away'?
This is my haven;
who shall take this solace from me?

PADRE GUARDIANO:
A te sia gloria, o Dio clemente,
padre dei miseri onnipossente.
A cui sgabello sono le sfere!
Il tuo volere si compirà! È fermo il voto?

V'accolga dunque Iddio.

LEONORA:
Bontà divina!

PADRE GUARDIANO:
Sol io saprò chi siate. Tra le rupi è uno
speco; ivi starete. Presso una fonte, al
settimo di, scarso cibo
porrovvi io stesso.

LEONORA:
V'andiamo.

PADRE GUARDIANO:
Melitone?
Tutti i fratelli con ardenti ceri,
dov' è l'ara maggiore,
nel tempio si raccolgan del Signore.

Sull'alba il piede all'eremo
solinga volgerete;
ma pria dal pane angelico
conforto all'alma avrete.

Le sante lane a cingere
ite, e sia forte il cor.
Sul nuovo calle a reggervi
v'assisterà il Signor.

LEONORA:

FATHER GUARDIANO:
Glory to Thee, O merciful God,
Omnipotent Father of the wretched,
whose footstools are the spheres!
Thy will be done!

May God then receive you!

LEONORA:
Divine compassion!

FATHER GUARDIANO:
Only I shall know who you are.
There is a cave among the rocks: there you
will stay. Near a spring, each seventh day, I
myself will set down a frugal meal.

LEONORA:
Let us go there.

FATHER GUARDIANO:
Melitone!
Let all the brothers, with lighted candles,
assemble at the high altar
in the temple of the Lord.

At dawn, you will make your way
alone to the hermitage;
but first you shall have
heavenly comfort from the holy bread.

Go, put on your holy robe,
and may your heart be firm.
The Lord will help you
to set forth on your new path.

LEONORA:

Tua grazia, o Dio.
Sorride alla regetta!
O, gaudio insolito!
Io son ribenedetta!
Già sento in me rinascere,

O God, Thy grace smiles upon the outcast!
Oh, unaccustomed joy!
I am blessed once more!
I feel my heart within me being reborn,
to new life. Sing praises,

a nuova vita il cor;
plaudite, o croi angelici,
mi perdonò il Signor.

o angelic chorus,
for the Lord has pardoned me.
I thank thee, O Lord.

The great door of the church opens, revealing the illuminated high altar. The organ is playing. Two files of monks proceed down the aisles, carrying lighted tapers. After them, the Father Superior, followed by Leonora in monk's habit.

PADRE GUARDIANO:
Il santo nome di Dio Signore
sia benedetto.

FATHER GUARDIANO:
Blessed be the holy name
of the Lord God.

FRA MELITONE e FRATELLI:
Sia benedetto.

FRA MELITONE and MONKS:
May it be blessed.

PADRE GUARDIANO:
Un'alma a piangere viene l'errore,
tra queste balze chiede ricetto;
il santo speco noi le schiudiamo.
V' è noto il loco?

FATHER GUARDIANO:
A soul has come to weep for its sin
and seeks sanctuary amid these mountains.
For this soul, we are opening the sacred
cave. You know the place?

FRA MELITONE e FRATELLI:
Lo conosciamo.

FRA MELITONE and MONKS:
We know it.

PADRE GUARDIANO:
A quell'asilo, sacro, inviolato, nessun si appressi.

FATHER GUARDIANO:
Let no one approach that holy, inviolate refuge.

FRA MELITONE e FRATELLI:
Obbediremo.

FRA MELITONE and MONKS:
We will obey.

PADRE GUARDIANO:
Il cinto umile non sia varcato che nel
divide.

FATHER GUARDIANO:
Nor shall the humble enclosure that
separates us be crossed

FRA MELITONE e FRATELLI:
Nol varcheremo.

MELITONE and MONKS:
We will not cross it.

PADRE GUARDIANO:
A chi il divieto
frangere osasse.
O di quest'alma
scoprir tentasse
nome o mistero:
maledizione!

FATHER GUARDIANO:
On him who would dare
to break this ban
or try to learn
the name or secret
of this soul,
a curse shall fall!

FRA MELITONE e FRATELLI:
Maledizione! Maledizione!
Il cielo fulmini, incenerisca,
l'empio mortale
se tanto ardisca;
su lui scatenisi
ogni elemento,
l'immonda cenere
ne sperda il vento.

MELITONE and MONKS:
A curse! A curse!
Let heaven hurl its thunderbolts and
consume the impious mortal
who would so dare.
Let all the elements
be showered upon him,
let his vile ashes
be scattered to the winds.

PADRE GUARDIANO:
Alzatevi e partite. Alcun vivente
più non vedrete. Dello speco il bronzo
ne avverta se periglio vi sovrasti,
o per voi giunto sia l'estremo giorno.
A confortarvi l'alma volerem
pria che a Dio faccia ritorno.

FATHER GUARDIANO:
Rise and depart. Henceforth you will see
no living soul. The bell of the cave
will warn us if danger threatens you,
or if your last hour has come.
Then we shall hasten to comfort your soul
before it returns to God.

LEONORA:

LEONORA:

La Vergine degli Angeli
vi copra del suo manto,
e voi protegga vigile
di Dio l'Angelo santo.

May Our Lady of the Angels
cover me in Her mantle,
and the Holy Angel of God
keep vigil to protect me.

Leonora sets off alone for the hermitage.
Padre Guadagno stretches out his arms towards her, signifying the Church's blessing.

END of ACT II

Act III — Scene 1:
The town of Velletri, Italy. It is night. Don Alvaro wears the uniform of a Spanish captain in the Royal Grenadiers. Soldiers play at cards.

SOLDATI:
Attenti al gioco, attenti, attenti al gioco, attenti.

SOLDIERS:
Keep your eyes on the game.

PRIMA SOLDATO:
Un asso a destra.

FIRST SOLDIER:
An ace on the right.

SEGUNDA SOLDATO:
Ho vinto.

SECOND SOLDIER:
I've won!

PRIMA SOLDATO:
Un tre alla destra. Cinque a manca.

FIRST SOLDIER:
A three on the right.

SEGUNDA SOLDATO:
Perdo.

SECOND SOLDIER:
A five on the left. I've lost!

ALVARO:
La vita è inferno all'infelice.
Invano morte desio!
Siviglia! Leonora!
Oh, rimembranza! Oh, notte
ch'ogni ben mi rapisti!

Sarò infelice eternanmente, è scritto.
Della natal sua terra il padre volle
spezzar l'estranio giogo,
e coll'unirsi
all'ultima dell'Incas la corona
cingere confidò.

Fu vana impresa.
in un carcere nacqui;
m'educava il deserto;
sol vivo perché ignota
e mia regale stirpe!

I miei parenti
sognaro un trono, e li destò la scure!
Oh, quando fine avran
le mie sventure!

ALVARO:
Life is a hell to the unfortunate.
In vain do I long for death.
Seville! Leonora!
Oh, memories! Oh, night
that robbed me of all joy!

I shall be unhappy forever — so it is written.
My father wished to shatter the foreign
yoke on his native land,
and by uniting himself
with the last of the Incas, he thought he
would assume the crown.

The attempt was in vain!
I was born in prison,
educated in the desert;
I live only because my royal birth
is known to none!

My parents
dreamed of a throne;
the axe awakened them!
Oh, when will my misfortunes end?

O tu che seno agli angeli
eternamente pura,
salisti bella, incolume
dalla mortal jattura,

Oh, you who have ascended,
forever pure, to the bosom of the angels,
lovely and untouched
by mortal sorrow.

Non iscordar di volgere
lo sguardo a me tapino,
che senza nome ed esule,
in odio del destino,
chiedo anelando,
ahi misero, la morte d'incontrar.

Do not forget to look down on me,
unhappy wretch,
who, nameless and exiled,
unfortunate that I am,
a victim of fate,
longingly seeks to find death!

Leonora mia, soccorrimi,
pietà del mio penar!
Pietà di me!

Leonora, help me,
have pity on my anguish.
Help me, have pity on me!

CARLOS:
Al tradimento!

CARLOS: *(in the distance)*
Treachery!

VOCI:
Muoia!

VOICES: *(in the distance)*
Let him die!

ALVARO:
Quali grida!

ALVARO:
What is that shouting?

CARLOS:
Aita!

CARLOS:
Help!

ALVARO:
Si soccorra.

ALVARO:
I must help.

VOCI:
Muoia! Muoia!

VOICES:
Kill him!

Don Alvaro runs off to investigate the cries and the clash of swords.
He returns with Don Carlos.

ALVARO:
Fuggir! Ferito siete?

ALVARO:
They've escaped. Are you wounded?

CARLOS:
No, vi debbo la vita.

CARLOS:
No. I owe my life to you.

ALVARO:
Chi erano?

ALVARO:
Who were they?

CARLOS:
Assassini.

CARLOS:
Assassins.

ALVARO:
Presso al campo così?

ALVARO:
So near camp?

CARLOS:
Franco dirò: fu alterco al gioco.

CARLOS:
I will be frank: it was a quarrel over cards.

ALVARO:
Comprendo, colà, a destra.

ALVARO:
I see! Over there to the right?

CARLOS:
Sì.

CARLOS:
Yes.

ALVARO:
Ma come, si nobile d'aspetto, a quella bisca scendeste?

ALVARO:
But how did you, so noble of bearing, become involved with that den of thieves?

CARLOS:
Nuovo sono.
Con ordini del general sol ieri giunsi; senza voi morto sarei.
Or dite a chi debbo la vita?

CARLOS:
I'm new here. I arrived with orders from the general only yesterday; without you I would now be dead.
Tell me, to whom do I owe my life?

ALVARO:
Al caso.

ALVARO:
To chance.

CARLOS:
Pria il mio nome dirò. (Non sappia il vero.)
Don Felice de Bornos, aiutante del duce.

CARLOS:
First, your name; (I must hide the truth!);
Don Felix de Bornos, aide to the commander.

ALVARO:
Io, Capitan dei Granatieri,
Don Federico Herreros.

ALVARO:
I am Don Federico Herreros,
captain of Grenadiers.

CARLOS:
La gloria dell'esercito!

CARLOS:
The pride of the army!

ALVARO:
Signore!

ALVARO:
Sir!

CARLOS:
Io l'amistà ne ambia; la chiedo e spero.

CARLOS:
I desire your friendship; I ask and hope for it.

ALVARO:
Io pure della vostra sarò fiero.

ALVARO:
And I shall be proud to have yours!

ALVARO e CARLO:
Amici in vita e in morte
il mondo ne vedrà.
Uniti in vita e in morte
entrambi troverà.

ALVARO and CARLOS: *(they shake hands)*
Friends in life and death!
The world shall see us.
united in life and death,
where it shall find us both.

VOCI INTERNO:
Andiamo, all'armi!

VOICES WITHIN:
To arms!

CARLOS:
Con voi scendere al campo d'onor,
emularne l'esempio potrò.

CARLOS:
By going to the field of honor with you,
I can emulate your example.

ALVARO:
Testimone del vostro valor
ammirarne le prove saprò.

ALVARO:
As witness of your courage,
I shall be able to admire its proof.

ALVARO ed CARLOS:
All'armi!

ALVARO and CARLOS:
To arms!

SOLDATI:
All'armi!

SOLDIERS:.
To arms!

Act III — Scene 2: Velletri, Italy. It is morning at the quarters of a senior officer of the Spanish army. The sounds of a nearby battle can be heard. An army surgeon and orderlies appear.

SOLDATI:
Arde la mischia.

SOLDIERS:
The battle is fierce!

CHIRURGO:
Prodi i granatieri!

SURGEON: *(looking through the telescope)*
The grenadiers are valiant!

SOLDATI:
Li guida Herreros.

SOLDIERS:
Herreros is leading them.

CHIRURGO:
Ciel! Ferito ei cadde!
Piegano i suoi!
L'aiutante li raccozza,
alla carica li guida!
Già fuggono i nemici.
I nostri han vinto!

SURGEON:
My God, he is wounded and has fallen!
His men are giving way!
His aide is rallying them,
leading them in a charge!
The enemy is on the run now.
Our men have won!

SOLDATI:
A Spagna gloria!

SOLDIERS:
Glory to Spain!

ALTRE SOLDATI:
Viva l'Italia!

OTHER SOLDIERS:
Long live Italy!

TUTTI:
Vittoria!

ALL:
Victory!

CHIRURGO:
Portan qui ferito il Capitano.

SURGEON:
They're bringing the Captain here, wounded.

Don Alvaro, wounded and unconscious, is brought in on a stretcher by four grenadiers. The surgeon and Don Carlos stand beside him.

CARLOS:
Piano, qui posi,
approntisi il mio letto.

CARLOS:
Gently - put him here - prepare my bed for him.

CHIRURGO:
Silenzio.

SURGEON:
Quiet!

CARLOS:
V'ha periglio?

CARLOS:
Is he in danger?

CHIRURGO:
La piaga che ha nel petto mi spaventa.

SURGEON:
The bullet in his chest causes me concern.

CARLOS:
Deh, il salvate.

CARLOS:
Oh, save him!

ALVARO:
Ove son?

ALVARO: *(gaining consciousness)*
Where am I?

CARLOS:
Presso l'amico.

CARLOS:
With your friend.

ALVARO:
Lasciatemi morire.

ALVARO:
Let me die.

CARLOS:
Vi salveran le nostre cure. Premio L'Ordine
vi sarà di Calatrava.

CARLOS:
Our treatment will save you. You will be awarded the Order of Calatrava.

ALVARO:
Di Calatrava! Mai! Mai!

ALVARO:
Of Calatrava! Never! Never!

CARLOS:
(Che! Inorridi di Calatrava al nome!)

CARLOS:
(What! You shudder at the name of Calatrava!)

ALVARO:
Amico...

ALVARO:
My friend...

CHIRURGO:
Se parlate...

SURGEON:
If you talk...

ALVARO
Un detto sol...

ALVARO:
One word only...

CARLOS:
Ven prego ne lasciate.

CARLOS: *(to the surgeon)*
Be good enough to leave us.

The surgeon withdraws to the background.
Don Alvaro beckons Don Carlos to come closer to him.

ALVARO:

ALVARO:

Solenne in quest'ora giurami dovete
far pago un mio voto.

You must swear to me, in this solemn hour,
to carry out a wish of mine.

CARLOS:
Lo giuro.

CARLOS:
I swear.

ALVARO:
Sul core cercate.

ALVARO:
Look above my heart.

CARLOS:
Una chiave.

CARLOS: *(He discovers a key)*
A key!

ALVARO:
Con essa trarrete
un piego celato!
L'affido all'onore,
colà v'ha un mistero
che meco morrà.
S'abbruci me spento.

ALVARO: *(pointing to a case)*
Take it with you,
and take out a hidden packet.
I entrust it to your honor.
Within it is a secret
which must die with me.
Burn it when I am dead.

CARLOS:
Lo giuro, sarà.

CARLOS:
It shall be done, I swear.

ALVARO:
Or muoio tranquillo;
vi stringo al cor mio.

ALVARO:
Now I can die in peace. I press you to my heart.

CARLOS:
Amico, fidate nel cielo!

CARLOS: *(embracing him, emotionally)*
My friend, trust in heaven. Farewell.

ALVARO e CARLOS:
Addio.

ALVARO and CARLOS:
Farewell.

The surgeon and orderlies set the wounded Don Alvaro on a bed.

CARLOS:
Morir! Tremenda cosa!
Sì intrepido, sì prode, ei pur morrà!
Uom singolar costui!
Tremò di Calatrava al nome.
A lui palese n' è forse il disonor?
Cielo! Qual lampo! S'ei fosse il seduttore?
Desso in mia mano, e vive!
Se m'ingannassi?
Questa chiave il dica.

CARLOS:
To die! A terrible thing, so fearless, so valiant, yet he must die!
A strange man, this!
He shuddered at the name of Calatrava!
Has he perhaps heard of our dishonor?
Heavens! A sudden thought!
What if he was the seducer?
And in my hands — alive!
But if I am wrong? This key will tell me!

Carlos opens the case and removes a sealed envelope.

Ecco i fogli! Che tento!

Here are the papers!

E la fè che giurai?
E questa vita che debbo al suo valor?
Anch'io lo salvo!
S'ei fosse quell' Indo
maledetto che macchiò il sangue mio?
Il suggello sì franga.
Niun qui mi vede.
No? Ben mi vegg'io!

What am I doing?
And the oath I swore? And I owe
my life yo his bravery?
But I saved him, too!
And what if he were the cursed Indian
who soiled my blood?
I will break the seal, no one can see me here.
No? But I can see myself.

Urna fatale del mio destino,
va, t'allontana, mi tenti in vano;
l'onor a tergere qui venni, e insano
d'un onta nuova nol macchierò.
Un giuro è sacro per l'uom d'onore;
que' fogli serbino il lor mistero.

Away with you, fatal urn of my destiny;
you tempt me in vain. I came here to
redeem my honor, and in my madness will
not stain it with this new shame.
An oath is sacred to a man of honor;
these papers shall keep their secret.

Disperso vada il mal pensiero
che all'atto indegno mi concitò.
E s'altra prova rinvenir potessi?
Vediam.

Perish the evil thought
that spurred me to the unworthy deed.
But if I could find some other proof?
Let's see.

Qui v'ha un ritratto.
Suggel non v'è, nulla ei ne disse,
Nulla promisi, s'apra dunque

Here is a portrait.
It has no seal. He said nothing about this.
I promised nothing. Let me open it then.

Ciel! Leonora!

Heavens! Leonora!

Don Alvaro è il ferito!
Ora egli viva, e di mia man poi muoia!

The wounded man is Don Alvaro!
Now let him live, and then die by my hand!

CHIRURGO:
Lieta novella, è salvo!

SURGEON: *(expressing joy)*
Good news; he's saved.

CARLOS:
È salvo! Oh gioia!

CARLOS:
He is saved! Oh joy!

Egli è salvo! Gioia immensa
che m'innondi il cor ti sento!
Potrò alfine il tradimento
sull'infame vendicar.

He is saved! What immense joy
I feel flooding my heart!
At last I can avenge
the betrayal on this vile wretch!

Leonora, ove t'ascondi?
Di': seguisti tra le squadre
chi del sangue di tuo padre
ti fe' il volto rosseggiar?

Leonora, where are you hiding?
Tell me, have you followed the man
into this camp who reddened your face
with your father's blood?

Ah, felice appien sarei
se potessi il brando mio
ambedue d'averno al dio
d'un sol colpo consacrar!

Ah, I should be overjoyed
if this sword of mine, with a single stroke,
could send them both forever,
below to the Prince of Darkness!

Act III — Scene 3: ***It is night at a military encampment near Velletri.***

SOLDATI:
Il campo esploriamo;
non s'ode rumor,
non brilla un chiarore;
in sonno profondo
sepolto ognun sta.

Compagni, inoltriamo,
il campo esploriamo,
fra poco la sveglia
suonare s'udrà.

SOLDIERS:
Comrades, let's stop
and explore the camp;
not a sound can be heard.
Not a glimmer of light shines;
everyone is buried in profound sleep.

Companions, let's advance
and explore the camp;
soon reveille
will be sounded.

Dawn is slowly breaking. Don Alvaro enters, deep in thought, followed by Don Carlos.

ALVARO:
Nè gustare m' è dato
un' ora di quiete.
Affranta è l'alma dalla lotta crudel.
Pace ed oblio indarno io chieggo al cielo.

ALVARO:
I am deprived of enjoying one hour of
peace; my soul is racked by the cruel strife.
In vain, I ask heaven
for peace and oblivion.

CARLOS:
Capitano.

CARLOS:
Captain.

ALVARO:
Chi mi chiama?
Voi, che si larghe cure mi prodigaste.

ALVARO:
Who calls me?
You who lavished such great care on me?

CARLOS:
La ferita vostra sanata è appieno?

CARLOS:
Is your wound fully healed?

ALVARO:
Sì.

ALVARO:
Yes.

CARLOS:
Forte?

CARLOS:
Are you strong?

ALVARO:
Quale prima.

ALVARO:
As before.

CARLOS:
Sosterreste un duel?

CARLOS:
Could you fight a duel?

ALVARO:
Con chi?

ALVARO:
With whom?

CARLOS:
Nemici non avete?

ALVARO:
Tutti ne abbiam, ma a stento comprendo.

CARLOS:
No? Messaggio non v'inviava
Don Alvaro, l'Indiano?

ALVARO:
Oh tradimento!
Sleale! Il segreto fu dunque violato?

CARLOS:
Fu illeso quel piego, l'effigie ha parlato.
Don Carlos di Vargas, tremate io sono.

ALVARO:
D'ardite minacce non m'agito al suono.

CARLOS:
Usciamo all'istante. Un deve morire.

ALVARO:
La morte disprezzo, ma duolmi inveire
contr'uom che per primo amistade
m'offria.

CARLOS:
No, no, profanato tal nome non sia.

ALVARO:
Non io, fu il destino,
che il padre v'ha ucciso.
Non io che sedussi
quell'angiol d'amore.
Ne guardano entrambi,
e dal paradiso
ch'io sono innocente
vi dicono al core.

CARLOS:
Adunque colei?

CARLOS:
Have you no enemies?

ALVARO:
We all have, but I hardly understand.

CARLOS:
No? Did the Indian Don Alvaro
send you no message?

ALVARO:
Oh, treachery!
Faithless man! So the secret was violated?

CARLOS:
That packet was unread; the portrait gave it
away. Tremble, I am Don Carlos de Vargas.

ALVARO:
I am agitated by the sound of violent threats.

CARLOS:
Come out at once: one of us must die.

ALVARO:
I scorn death, but it grieves me
to revile one who at first offered me
friendship.

CARLOS:
No, no, let that name not be profaned.

ALVARO:
It was not I, but destiny,
that killed your father;
nor did I seduce
that angel of love.
They both look down on us,
and from heaven
they tell you in your heart
that I am innocent.

CARLOS:
And she?

ALVARO:
La notte fatale
io caddi per doppia
ferita mortale;
guaritone, un anno
in traccia ne andai,
ahimè, ch'era spenta
Leonora trovai.

ALVARO:
That fatal night,
I fell,
with two grievous wounds.
When I recovered,
I searched for a year.
Alas, I found
that Leonora was no more!

CARLOS:
Menzogna, menzogna!
La suora ospitavala antica parente.
vi giunsi, ma tardi.

CARLOS:
You lie, you lie!
An old relative gave my sister shelter;
I went to her, but it was too late.

ALVARO:
Ed ella?

ALVARO:
And she?

CARLOS:
Fuggente.

CARLOS:
She fled.

ALVARO:
E vive! Ella vive, gran Dio!

ALVARO:
And is alive! She lives, great God!!

CARLOS:
Sì, vive.

CARLOS:
Yes, she lives.

ALVARO:
Don Carlo, amico, il fremito
ch'ogni mia fibra scuote,
vi dica che quest' anima
infame esser non puote.
Vive! Gran Dio, quel angelo.

ALVARO:
Don Carlos, my friend, let the tremor
that shakes my every fiber
tell you that my soul
is incapable of baseness.
She lives! Great God, that angel!

CARLOS:
Ma in breve morirà. Ella vive, ma in breve morirà.

CARLOS:
But soon she shall die. She lives, but soon shall die.

ALVARO:

ALVARO:

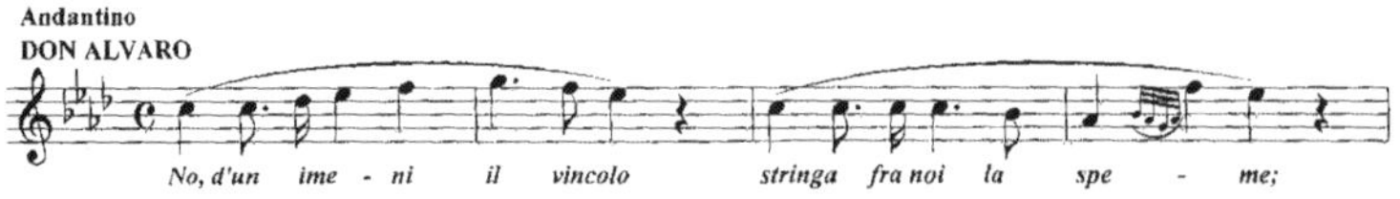

No, d'un imene il vincolo
stringa fra noi la speme;
e s'ella vive, insieme cerchiamo ove fuggì.

No, let the hope of Hymen's bond
draw us together; and if she is alive,
let us together seek where she has fled to.

Giuro che illustre origine e
equale a voi mi rende,
e che il mio stemma splende
come rifulge il dì.

I swear that a noble origin
makes me your equal,
and that my escutcheon
shines as brightly as the day.

CARLOS:
Stolto! Fra noi dischiudesi
insanguinato avello.
Come chiamar fratello
chi tanto a me rapì?
D'eccelsa o vile origine.
È d'uopo ch'io vi spegna,
e dopo voi l'indegna
che il sangue suo tradì.

CARLOS:
Fool! Between us a bloody, wide-mouthed
sepulcher awaits us.
How can I call brother
one who has robbed me of everything?
Whether your origin is noble or base,
I must kill you,
and after you, that worthless creature,
who betrayed her own flesh and blood.

ALVARO:
Che dite?

ALVARO:
What are you saying?

CARLOS:
Ella morrà.

CARLOS:
She shall die.

ALVARO:
Tacete!

ALVARO:
Do not say that.

CARLOS:
Il giuro a Dio: morrà l'infame.

CARLOS:
I swear it before God: the shameful one
shall die.

ALVARO:
Voi pria cadrete nel fatal certame.

ALVARO:
You shall fall first in mortal combat.

CARLOS:
Morte! Ov'io non cada esanime
Leonora giungerò
tinto ancor del vostro sangue
questo acciar le immergerò.

CARLOS:
Death! Before I fall lifeless
I will reach Leonora
and plunge this blade into her,
a blade still reddened with your blood.

ALVARO:

ALVARO:

Morte! Sì! Col brando mio
un sicario ucciderò;
il pensier volgete a Dio.
L'ora vostra alfin suonò.

Death, yes! With my sword
I will kill a murderer.
Turn your thoughts to God;
your time has fnally run out.

ALVARO e CARLOS:
A morte! Andiam!

ALVARO and CARLOS:
Let us go! We go to death!

SOLDATI:
Fermi! Arrestate!

SOLDIERS:
Stop! Sheathe your weapons!

CARLOS:
No, la sua vita o la mia, tosto.

CARLOS: *(furiously)*
No. His life or mine, at once.

SOLDATI:
Lunge di qua si tragga.

SOLDIERS:
Lead them away from here.

ALVARO:
(Forse del ciel l'aita a me soccorre.)

ALVARO:
(Perhaps heaven is assisting me.)

CARLOS:
Colui morrà!

CARLOS:
He shall die!

SOLDATI:
Vieni!

SOLDIERS: *(to Carlos)*
Come!

CARLOS:
Carnefice del padre mio!

CARLOS: *(to Don Alvaro)*
My father's murderer!

They draw their swords and fight furiously. The camp patrol drags Carlos away.

ALVARO:
Or che mi resta? Pietoso Iddio,
tu ispira, illumina il mio pensier.
Al chiostro, all'eremo, ai santi altari
l'oblio, la pace chiegga il guerrier.

ALVARO:
Now what is left me? Merciful God,
inspire and enlighten my thoughts.
Let the warrior seek peace and oblivion
in the cloister, at the holy altars.

A roll of drums and a blare of trumpets signal reveille. As the sun rises, Spanish and Italian soldiers come out of their tents and busily begin to clean rifles, swords, and uniforms. Military cadets play at dice on the drums. Vivandières sell drinks, fruit and bread. From the top of a booth, Preziosilla is telling fortunes.

SOLDATI:
Lorchè pifferi e tamburi
Par che assordino la terra,
Siam felici, ch' è la guerra
Gioia e vita al militar.

SOLDIERS:
When fifes and drums
seem to deafen the earth
we are happy, for to the soldier
war is life and joy.

Vita gaia, avventurosa,
cui non cal doman nè ieri,
ch' ama tutti i suoi pensieri
sol nell'oggi concentrar.

A gay, adventurous life
for one who cares not for tomorrow,
or yesterday, and loves to
live for today!

PREZIOSILLA:
Venite all'indovina,
ch' è giunta di lontano,
e puote a voi l'arcano
futuro decifrar.

PREZIOSILLA:
Come to the fortune-teller,
who has come from afar,
and can interpret the mysterious future
of the soldiers.

Correte a lei d'intorno,
la mano le porgete,
le amanti apprenderete
se fide vi restâr.

Come, gather round her,
show her your hands!
You will learn if your sweethearts
are remaining true to you.

TUTTI:
Andiamo all'indovina,
la mano le porgiamo,
le belle udir possiamo
se fide a voi restâr.

ALL:
Go to the fortune-teller,
give her your hands,
you will learn if your fair ones
are remaining true to you.

PREZIOSILLA:
Chi vuole il paradiso
s'accenda di valore,
e il barbaro invasore
s'accinga a debellar.

PREZIOSILLA:
He who longs for paradise
must burn with valor
and prepare to drive out
the barbarous invader.

Avanti, avanti, avanti,
predirvi sentirete
qual premio coglierete
dal vostro battagliar. Ah!

Come, come, come,
you shall hear me predict
what prize you will win
from your fighting. Ah!

SOLDATI:
Avanti, avanti, avanti,
predirci sentiremo
qual premio coglieremo
dal nostro battagliar.

SOLDIERS:
Go on, go on, go on,
you shall hear her predict
what prize you will win
from your fighting.

SOLDATI:
Qua, vivandiere, un sorso.

SOLDIERS:
Here, girls, pour me a drink.

UN SOLDATO:
Alla salute nostra!

SOLDIER:
To our health!

TUTTI:
Viva!

ALL:
Good health!

UN SOLDATO:
A Spagna ed all'Italia unite!

SOLDIER:
To a united Spain and Italy!

TUTTI:
Evviva!

ALL:
Good health!

PREZIOSILLA:
Al nostro eroe Don Federico Herreros!

PREZIOSILLA:
To our hero, Don Frederico Herreros!

TUTTI:
Viva! Viva!

ALL:
Hurrah! Hurrah!

UN ALTRO SOLDATO:
Ed al suo degno amico Don Felice de Bornos.

SOLDIER:
And to his noble friend Don Felix de Bornos!

TUTTI:
Viva, viva!

ALL:
Hurrah! Hurrah!

Trabuco, the peddler, bears a tray of cheap merchandise.

TRABUCO:
A buon mercato chi vuol comprare?
Forbici, spille, sapon perfetto!
Io vendo e compro qualunque oggetto,
concludo a pronti qualunque affar.

TRABUCO:
Who wants to buy cheap? Scissors, pins, beautiful soap.
I buy and sell anything, and strike a deal straight away.

UN SOLDATO:
Ho qui un monile; quanto mi dai?

SOLDIER:
I've a bracelet; what'll you give me for it?

ALTRO SOLDATO:
V' è una collana. Se vuoi la vendo.

ANOTHER SOLDIER:
Here's a necklace. I'll sell it if you.

UN SOLDATO:
Questi orecchini, li pagherai?

SOLDIER:
What'll you pay for these earrings?

TUTTI:
Vogliamo vendere.

ALL:
We want to sell.

TRABUCO:
Ma quanto vedo tutto è robaccia, brutta robaccia!

TRABUCO:
But as far as I can see it's all trash, worthless trash!

TUTTI:
Tale, o furfante, è la tua faccia.

ALL:
Just like your face, you rogue.

TRABUCO:
Pure aggiustiamoci, per ogni pezzo
do trenta soldi.

TRABUCO:
Still, let's agree; I'll give you thirty soldi for each article.

TUTTI:
Da ladro è il prezzo.

ALL:
That's plain robbery!

TRABUCO:
Ih! Quanta furia! C'intenderemo. Qualch' altro soldo v'aggiungeremo. Date qua, subito!

TRABUCO:
Hey, what fury! Let's agree. We'll add a few more soldi. Give me the things, quickly!

SOLDATI:
Purchè all'istante venga il denaro bello e sonante.

SOLDIERS:
On condition the money's forthcoming, shiny and ringing.

TRABUCO:
Prima la merce, qua, colle buone.

TRABUCO:
First the goods, here, one at a time.

SOLDATI:
A te.

SOLDIERS: *(handing him the objects)*
Here you are.

TRABUCO:
A te, a te, benone.

TRABUCO:
Here you are, good!.

TUTTI:
Sì, sì, ma vattene!

ALL:
Yes, but now be off with you!

TRABUCO:
Che buon affare!
A buon mercato chi vuol comprare?

TRABUCO:
That was good business!
Who wants to buy cheap?

Trabuco goes to the other side of the camp to do his trading.
Begging peasants and conscripts appear, all weeping.

CONTADINI:
Pane, pan per carità!
Tetti e campi devastati
n'ha la guerra, ed affamati
cerchiam pane per pietà.

PEASANTS:
Bread, bread, for pity's sake!
The war has destroyed
our homes and fields. We are starving,
and beg for bread, for mercy's sake!

RECLUTE:
Povere madri deserte nel pianto
per dura forza dovemmo lasciar.
Della beltà n'han rapiti all'incanto,
a' nostre case vogliamo tornar.

CONSCRIPTS:
They used brute force to make us leave
our poor mothers, deserted and in tears.
We've been torn away from all we love,
and we want to go back home.

VIVANDIERE:
Non piangete, giovanotti,
per le madri, per le belle;
v'ameremo quai sorelle,
vi sapremo consolar.

VIVANDIERES: *(offering drinks)*
Don't cry, lads,
for your mothers and sweethearts.
We will love you like sisters,
and we know how to console you.

Certo il diavolo non siamo;
quelle lagrime tergete,
al passato, ben vedete,
ora è inutile pensar.

Certainly we're not devils.
So dry your tears.
As you can see, it's no use
pondering about the past.

PREZIOSILLA:
Che vergogna! Su, coraggio!
Bei figliuoli, siete pazzi?
Se piangete quai ragazzi
vi farete corbellar.

PREZIOSILLA: *(grabbing a couple)*
Shame on you! Come, be brave!
Handsome lads, are you mad?
If you cry like babies,
you'll be laughed at.

Un' occhiata a voi d'intorno,
e scommetto che indovino,
ci sarà più d'un visino
che sapravvi consolar.
Su, coraggio, coraggio, coraggio!

Take a look around you;
I'll bet you can guess
there'll be more
than one pretty face
that will be able to console you.

The vivandières brazenly take the conscripts by the arms and dance with them. Soon the confusion and noise reach their heights.

TUTTI:
Nella guerra è la follia
che dee il campo rallegrar;
viva, viva la pazzia
che qui sola ha da regnar!

ALL:
In war it's foolery
that must enliven the camp.
Three cheers for frivolity,
which alone should reign here!

Fra Melitone appears. He becomes caught up in the whirl and dances with vivandières.

FRA MELITONE:
Toh! Toh! Poffare il mondo! Che tempone!
Corre ben l'avventura! Anch'io ci sono.
Venni di Spagna a medicar terite,
ed alme a mendicar.

MELITONE:
Whew! Good gracious, what a world!
What are things coming to? A fine thing!
Here I am; I came from Spain to heal
wounds and appeal for souls.

Che vedo? È questo un campo di Cristiani,
o siete Turchi?
Dove s'è visto berteggiar la santa domenica
così?
Ben più faccenda le bottiglie vi dan che le
battaglie!

What do I see? Is this a Christian camp, or
are you Turks?
Where was such derision of the holy
Sabbath ever seen?
You're more concerned with bottles than
with battles!

E invece di vestir cenere e sacco
qui si tresca con Venere, con Bacco?
Il mondo è fatto una casa di pianto;
ogni convento ora è covo del vento!
I santuari spelonche diventar di sanguinari;
perfino i tabernacoli di Cristo fatti son
ricettacoli del tristo.

And instead of donning sackcloth and ashes,
here you're involved with Venus and Bacchus.
The world has become a vale of tears;
every monastery now is a den of empty air!
Sanctuaries have become the lairs of the
sanguinary; even Christ's tabernacles
have been made to receive villains.

Tutto va a soqquadro. E la ragion? La ragion?
Pro peccata vestra: pei vostri peccati.

Everything's topsy-turvy. And why?
Because of sinners vice.

SOLDATI ITALIANI:
Ah, frate, frate!

ITALIAN SOLDIERS:
Oh, brother, brother!

FRA MELITONE:
Voi le feste calpestate, rubate,
bestemmiate.

MELITONE:
You profane the feast days,
you rob, you blaspheme.

SOLDATI ITALIANI:
Togone infame!

ITALIAN SOLDIERS:
You are a villain in monk's attire!

SOLDATI SPAGNUOLI:
Segui pur, padruccio.

SPANISH SOLDIERS:
Go on, old father!

FRA MELITONE:
E membri e capi siete d'una stampa:
Tutti eretici.
Tutti, tutti cloaca di peccati,
e finchè il mondo
puzzi di tal pece
non isperi la terra alcuna pace.

MELITONE:
Limbs and head, you're all alike,
all heretics,
all sewers of iniquity,
and as long as the world stinks of such
pitch, let the earth not hope for any peace.
With such pitch there's no peace.

SOLDATI ITALIANI:
Dàlli! Dàlli!

ITALIAN SOLDIERS: *(crowding him)*
Let him have it!

SOLDATI SPAGNUOLI:
Scappa! Scappa!

SPANISH SOLDIERS: *(defending him)*
Run away, run away!

SOLDATI ITALIANI:
Dàlli! Dàlli sulla cappa!

ITALIAN SOLDIERS:
Let him have it. On is head!

The Italian soldiers try to flog Fra Melitone, but he manages to escape.

PREZIOSILLA e CORO:
Lasciatelo chi'ei vada.
Far guerra ad un cappuccio! Bella impresa!
Non m'odon? Sia il tamburo sua difesa.

Rataplan, rataplan, della gloria
nel soldato ritempra l'ardor;
Rataplan, rataplan, di vittoria
questo suono è segnal percursor!

Rataplan, rataplan, or le schiere
son guidate raccolte a pugnar!

PREZIOSILLA and CHORUS:
Let him go! Beating a monk! A fine thing!
They won't hear me?
Then let the drum save him.

Rataplan, rataplan, strengthens
the love of glory in the soldier;
rataplan, rataplan, the sound
that signals victory to come!

Rataplan, rataplan, the ranks are forming
and are led to combat!

Rataplan, rataplan, le bandiere
del nemico si veggon piegar!
Rataplan, pim, pam, pum, inseguite
chi la terga, fuggendo, voltò.

Rataplan, rataplan, the enemy's flag
is seen to retreat!
Rataplan, plan, pim, pum, pum, pursue
those who turn tail and flee!

Rataplan, le gloriose ferite
col trionfo il destin coronò.
Rataplan, rataplan, la vittoria
più rifulge de' figli al valor!

Destiny has crowned your glorious wounds
with triumph.
Rataplan, rataplan, the victory of one's
country shines brighter for her sons' gallantry.

Rataplan, rataplan, la vittoria
al guerriero conquista ogni cor.
Rataplan, rataplan, rataplan!

Rataplan, rataplan, victory
wins every heart for the soldier.
Rataplan, rataplan, rataplan!

All the soldiers pretend to fire rifles, and then rush off.

END of ACT III

Act IV — Scene 1:
Inside the monastery of Our Lady of the Angels, in the vicinity of Hornachuelos. The Father Superior is gravely pacing backand forth while reading his breviary. A crowd of beggars appear; they carry crude bowls, pots and dishes.

MENDICANTI: Fate, la carità, andarcene dobbiam, andarcene dobbiamo, Andarcene dobbiam, la carità, la carità!	**BEGGARS:** Give us charity, we've been waiting for an hour! We must be on our way. Charity!

Fra Melitone appears, wearing a broad white apron. With the assistance of a lay brother, ther carry in a large cauldron.

FRA MELITONE: Che? Siete all'osteria? Quieti!	**MELITONE:** What? Are you at the inn? Quietly!
MENDICANTI: Qui, presto a me, presto a me.	**BEGGARS:** *(pushing and shoving for soup)* Here, quick, give me some.
FRA MELITONE: Quieti, quieti, quieti, quieti.	**MELITONE:** Quietly, quietly!
MENDICANTI: Quante porzioni a loro! Tutto vorrian per sè. N'ebbe già tre Maria!	**BEGGARS:** They're getting so many portions! They want the lot for themselves. Maria's had three helpings already!
UNA DONNA: Quattro a me.	**A WOMAN:** *(to Fra Melitone)* Four for me.
MENDICANTI: Quattro a lei!	**BEGGARS:** Four for her!
DONNA: Sì, perchè ho sei figliouli.	**WOMAN:** Yes, because I've six children.
FRA MELITONE: E perchè sei figliouli.	**MELITONE:** And why have you got six?
DONNA: Perché il mandò Iddio.	**WOMAN:** Because the good Lord sent them.
FRA MELITONE: Sì, Dio, Dio. Non li avreste se al par di me voi pure la schiena per coteste con aspra disciplina, e più le notti intere passaste recitando Rosari e Miserere.	**MELITONE:** Yes, of course, it was the good Lord. You wouldn't have them if, like me, with harsh discipline you scourged your back, and moreover spent whole nights reciting Rosaries and Misereres.

PADRE GUARDIANO:
Fratel.

FRA MELITONE:
Ma tai pezzenti son di fecondità
davvero spaventosa.

PADRE GUARDIANO:
Abbiate carità.

MENDICANTI:
Un po' di quel fondaccio ancora ne donate.

FRA MELITONE:
Il ben di Dio, bricconi, fondaccio voi chiamate?

MENDICANTI:
A me, padre a me, a me, a me.

FRA MELITONE:
Oh, andatene in malora,
o il ramajuol sul capo
v'aggiusto bene or ora
io perdo la pazienza!

PADRE GUARDIANO:
Carità.

LE DONNE:
Più carità ne usava il padre Raffael.

FRA MELITONE:
Sì, sì, man in otto giorni
avutone abbastanza
di poveri e minestra,
restò nella sua stanza,
e scaricò la soma
sul dosso a Melitone.
E poi con tal canaglia
Usar dovrò le buone?

PADRE GUARDIANO:
Soffrono tanto i poveri. La carità è un dovere.

FATHER SUPERIOR:
Brother.

MELITONE:
But those beggars are really
dreadfully prolific.

FATHER SUPERIOR:
Be charitable.

BEGGARS:
Give us a drop more of those dregs.

MELITONE:
You rascals, you call these dregs manna from heaven?

BEGGARS:
Me, Father, me, me.

MELITONE:
Oh, go to blazes,
or with this ladle,
I'll give you one right on your head
with this ladle right now!
I'm losing patience!

FATHER SUPERIOR:
Be kind to them!

WOMEN:
Father Raphael was kinder to us.

MELITONE:
Yes, yes, but in a week
he'd had enough
of the poor and the soup
and stayed in his room,
unloading the burden
on to Melitone's shoulders.
Anyway, must I treat
such rabble gently?

FATHER SUPERIOR:
The poor suffer so much, and charity is a

FRA MELITONE:
Carità, con costoro
che il fanno per mestiere?
Che un campanile abbattere
co' pugni sarien buoni,
che dicono fondaccio,
fondaccio il ben di Dio.
Bricconi, bricconi, bricconi!

.

MENDICANTI:
Oh, il padre Raffaele! Era un angelo!
Un santo!

FRA MELITONE:
Non mi seccate tanto!

MENDICANTI:
Sì, sì, un santo!

FRA MELITONE:
Il resto, a voi prendetevi,
non voglio più parole.
Fuori di qua, lasciatemi,
Sì, fuori al sole, al sole,
Lasciatemi! Pezzenti più di Lazzaro,
sacchi di pravità.
Via, via bricconi, al diavolo,
Toglietevi di qua;

MENDICANTI:
Oh, il padre Raffaele!
Era un angel! Era un santo!

FRA MELITONE:
Auf! Pazienza non v'ha che basti!

PADRE GUARDIANO:
Troppa dal Signor non ne aveste.
Facendo carità un dover s'adempie
da render fiero un angiol.

FRA MELITONE:
Che al mio posto in tre di finirebbe
col minestrar de' schiaffi.

PADRE GUARDIANO:
Tacete; umil sia Meliton, nè soffra se veda
preferisi Raffaele.

duty.

MELITONE:
Charity for people
who make a living from it?
Who'd be happy
to knock down a bell-tower
with his fists,
and call this manna from heaven dregs?
Rogues and rascals!

BEGGARS:
Oh, Father Raphael. He was an angel,
a saint!

MELITONE:
Stop bothering me!

BEGGARS:
Yes, a saint!

MELITONE:
Here, take what's left;
I don't want to hear another word.
Get out of here, leave me, yes,
and out you go into the sun.
Leave me! You beggars are worse than
Lazarus, sacks of depravity.
Be off, rascals, to the devil with you,
get out of here!

BEGGARS:
Oh, Father Raphael!
He was an angel, a saint!

MELITONE:
Ouf! There's never enough patience for this.

FATHER SUPERIOR:
The Lord didn't give you too much of it.
To give charity is to fulfill a duty
that would make any angel proud.

MELITONE:
Who, after three days in my job, would end
by ladling out blows.

FATHER SUPERIOR:
Hush! Melitone must be humble and not

FRA MELITONE:
Io? No, amico gli son, ma ha certi gesti,
parla da sè, ha cert'occhi.

PADRE GUARDIANO:
Son le preci, il digiuno.

FRA MELITONE:
Ier nell'orto lavorava cotanto stralunato,
che scherznado dissi: Padre, un mulatto
parmi.
Guardommi bieco, strinse le pugna, e...

PADRE GUARDIANO:
Ebbene?

FRA MELITONE:
Quando cadde sul campanil la folgore,
ed usciva fra la tempesta, gli gridai: mi
sembre Indian selvaggio
un urlo cacciò che mi gelava.

PADRE GUARDIANO:
Che v'ha a ridir?

FRA MELITONE:
Nulla, ma il guardo e penso, narraste,
che il demonio qui stette un tempo
in abito da frate.
Gli fosse il padre Raffael parente?

PADRE GUARDIANO:
Giudizi temerari, il ver narrai, ma n'ebbe il
Superior rivelazione allora, io, no.

FRA MELITONE:
Ciò è vero! Ma strano è molto il padre!
La ragione?

PADRE GUARDIANO:
Del mondo i disinganni,
l'assidua penitenza,
le veglie, l'astineza
quell'anima, quell'anima turbâr.

irritated to see Raphael preferred to him.

MELITONE:
Me? No. I'm his friend, but he has a certain
look when he talks to himself.

FATHER SUPERIOR:
It's the prayers and the fasting.

MELITONE:
Yesterday in the kitchen garden he was
working so furiously that in jest I said,
"Father, you're working like a black."
He glared at me, and clenched his fists, and...

FATHER SUPERIOR:
Well?

MELITONE:
When lightning struck the belfry, and he
went out into the storm, I called after him,
"You're like a wild Indian!" He let out
a howl that froze my blood.

FATHER SUPERIOR:
Why is that worth repeating?

MELITONE:
Nothing, but I look at him and think;
you told us that the devil
once stayed here in monk's clothing.
Could Father Raphael be a relative of his?

FATHER SUPERIOR:
Rash judgments; I spoke the truth, but it was
revealed to the Father Superior, not to me.

MELITONE:
That's true, but the father's very odd.
Why is it?

FATHER SUPERIOR:
Disillusionment with the world,
assiduous penance,
vigils and abstinence,
are all troubling his mind.

FRA MELITONE:
Sarrano i disinganni,
l'assidua penitenza,
le veglie, l'astinenza
che il capo gli guastâr!

MELITONE:
It'll be the disillusionment,
assiduous penance,
vigils and abstinence,
that have addled his brain!

PADRE GUARDIANO:
Giunge qualcuno, aprite.

FATHER SUPERIOR:
Someone has come. Open the door.

The Father Superior exits. Don Carlos, enveloped in a large cloak, enters imperiously.

CARLOS:
Siete il portiere?

CARLOS: *(haughtily)*
Are you the doorkeeper?

FRA MELITONE:
È goffo ben costui!
Se apersi, parmi....

MELITONE:
(He's a dolt!)
As I just opened it, I should think...

CARLOS:
Il padre Raffaele?

CARLOS:
Father Raphael?

FRA MELITONE:
(Un altro!)
Due ne abbiamo; l'un di Porcuna, grasso,
sordo come una talpa. Un altro scarno,
bruno, occhi, (ciel, quali occhi!)
Voi chiedete?

MELITONE:
(Another one!)
We have two of them —one from Porcuna,
fat, deaf as a post; the other lean,
darks eyes (Heaven, what eyes!)
Which one do you want?

CARLOS:
Quell dell'inferno.

CARLOS:
The one from hell.

FRA MELITONE:
(È desso!) E chi gli annuncio?

MELITONE:
(That's him.) And who shall I announce?

CARLOS:
Un cavalier.

CARLOS:
A gentleman.

FRA MELITONE:
Qual boria! È un mal arnese.

MELITONE: *(as he departs)*
(What arrogance! An unpleasant fellow!)

CARLOS:
Invano Alvaro ti celasti al mondo,
e d'ipocrita veste scudo facesti alla viltà.
Del chiostro ove t'ascondi m'additar la via
l'odio e la sete di vendetta; alcuno qui non
sarà che ne divida.

CARLOS:
In vain, Alvaro, you hid from the world, and
hypocritically made a monk's habit a shield
for your baseness. Hatred and the thirst for
revenge have pointed me here. There will be
no one here to intervene between us.

Il sangue, solo il tuo sangue può lavar
l'oltraggio che macchiò l'onor mio,
e tutto il verserò. Lo giuro a Dio.

Blood, your blood alone, can wash away
the outrage that stained my honor;
and I will spill it all, I swear to God!

Don Alvaro enters, dressed in a monk's habit.

ALVARO:
Fratello.

ALVARO:
Brother.

CARLOS:
Riconoscimi.

CARLOS:
Know who I am!

ALVARO:
Don Carlo! Voi, vivente!

ALVARO:
Don Carlos! You, alive!

CARLOS:
Da un lustro ne vo' in traccia,
ti trovo finalmente;
col sangue sol cancellasi
l'infamia ed il delitto.

Ch'io ti punisca è scritto
sul libro del destin.
Tu prode fosti, or monaco,
un 'arma qui non hai.
Deggio il tuo sangue spargere.
Scegli, due ne portai.

CARLOS:
For five years I have searched for you;
at last I've found you.
Only with blood can the disgrace
and the crime be wiped out.

That I should punish you
is written in the book of fate.
Once you were brave;
now, as a monk, you have no sword.
I must spill your blood:
choose, for I have brought two.

ALVARO:
Vissi nel mondo, intendo;
Or queste vesti, l'eremo,
dicon che i falli ammendo,
che penitente è il cor.
Lasciatemi.

ALVARO:
Once I lived in that world, so I understand;
now this robe, this retreat, they show that I
am making amends for my misdeeds,
and that my heart is penitent.
Leave me!

CARLOS:
Difendere quel sajo, nè il deserto.
Codardo, te nol possono.

CARLOS:
Neither that monk'' habit nor this solitary
place can protect you, coward!

ALVARO:
Codardo! Tale asserto.
No, no! Assistimi, Signore!

ALVARO:
Coward! You dare to say.
Ah, no! Help me, Lord!

Le minaccie, i fieri accenti,
portin seco in preda i venti;
perdonatemi, pietà,
o fratel, pietà, pietà!

Let threats and violent words
be carried away by the winds.
Forgive me; have pity,
brother, have pity!

A che offendere cotanto
chi fu solo sventurato?
Deh, chiniam la fronte al fato!

Why insult one who was only unfortunate?
Come, let us bow before fate;
brother, have pity!

CARLOS:
Tu contamini tal nome.
Una suora mi lasciasti
che tradita abbandonasti
all'infamia, al disonor.

CARLOS:
You sully such a word.
Ah! You left to me a sister
who betrayed you and abandoned
you to infamy and dishonor.

ALVARO:
No, non fu disonorata,
Ve lo giura un sacerdote!
Sulla terra l'ho adorata
come in cielo amar sì puote.
L'amo ancora, e s'ella m'ama
più non brama questo cor.

ALVARO:
No, she was not dishonored,
I swear it to you as a priest.
On earth, I adored her
as one can love in heaven.
I love her still; if she still loves me,
my heart asks for nothing more.

CARLOS:
Non sì placa il mio furore
per mendace e vile accento;
l'arme impugna ed al cimento
scendi meco, o traditor.

CARLOS:
My rage is not to be placated
by lying and cowardly words;
take up a sword, traitor,
and do battle with me!

ALVARO:
Se i rimorsi, il pianto omai
non vi parlano per me,
qual nessun mi vide mai,
io mi prostro al vostro piè!

ALVARO:
If remorse and tears
no longer plead for me,
I will do what no one has ever seen me do:
throw myself at your feet!

CARLOS:
Ah la macchia del tuo stemma
or provasti con quest'atto!

CARLOS:
Ah, by this act, you have proved the stain
on your escutcheon.

ALVARO:
Desso splende più che gemma.

ALVARO:
It shines brighter than a jewel.

CARLOS:
Sangue il tinge di mulatto.

CARLOS:
It is tinted with your half-breed's blood.

ALVARO:
Per la gola voi mentite!
A me un brando! Un brando, uscite!

ALVARO:
You lie in your throat!
Give me a sword, a sword, lead on!

CARLOS:
Finalmente!

CARLOS:
At last!

ALVARO:
No, l'inferno non trionfi. Va, riparti.

ALVARO: *(He throws down his sword)*
No, the devil shall not triumph. Go, leave me.

CARLOS:
Ti fai dunque di me scherno?

CARLOS:
So you mock me?

ALVARO:
Va.

ALVARO:
Go.

CARLOS:
S'ora meco misurarti,
o vigliacco, non hai core,
ti consacro al disonore.

CARLOS: *(he slaps his face)*
If not now, coward, you lack courage
to measure swords with me,
I condemn you to dishonor.

ALVARO:
Ah, segnasti la tua sorte!
Morte.

ALVARO: *(in a fury)*
Ah, now you have sealed your fate!
Death!

CARLOS:
Morte! A entrambi morte!

CARLOS:
Death, death to both!

CARLOS e ALVARO:
Ah! Vieni a morte, a morte andiam!

CARLOS and ALVARO:
Ah! Death, come forth to death! Let us go!

Act IV — Scene 2:

A valley amid precipitous rocks, traversed by a stream. There is a cave, above which is a bell that can be rung from within. The sun is descending. The scene darkens slowly; the moon appears, extremely bright. Donna Leonora, pale and worn, emerges from the cave in a state of great agitation.

LEONORA:

LEONORA:

Pace, pace, mio Dio!
Cruda sventura
m'astringe, ahimè, a languir;
come il di primo
da tant'anni dura
profondo il mio soffrir.

Peace, peace, O God!
Cruel misfortune comes down.
and compels me, alas, to languish;
my suffering has lasted for so many years,
as profound as on the first day.
Peace, peace, O God!

L'amai, gli è ver!
Ma di beltà e valore
cotanto Iddio l'ornò.
Che l'amo ancor.

Nè togliermi dal core
l'immagin sua saprò.
Fatalità! Fatalità! Fatalità!
Un delitto disgiunti n'ha quaggiù!

Alvaro, io t'amo.
E su nel cielo è scritto:
non ti vedrò mai più!
Oh Dio, Dio, fa ch'io muoia;
che la calma può darmi morte sol.

Invan la pace qui sperò quest'alma
in preda a tanto duol.
Misero pane, a prolungarmi vieni
la sconsolata vita.
Ma chi giunge?
Chi profanare ardisce il sacro loco?
Maledizione! Maledizione! Maledizione!

I loved him, it is true!
But God had blessed him
with such beauty and courage,
that I still love him.

And I cannot erase his image
from my heart.
Fatal destiny!
A crime has divided us down here!

Alvaro, I love you,
and in heaven above it is written
that I shall never see you again!
O God, God, let me die, for only death
can bring me peace.

In vain, my soul sought peace here,
but I am a victim of so much woe.
Wretched bread, you come to prolong
my inconsolable life.
But who dares to come here,
to profane this sacred retreat?
A curse! A curse!

Leonora quickly enters the cave. The clash of swords is heard in the distance.

CARLOS:
Io muoio! Confessione! L'alma salvate.

ALVARO:
E questo ancora sangue d'un Vargas.

CARLOS:
Confessione!

ALVARO:
Maledetto io sono. Ma qui presso è un eremita. A confortar correte un uom che muor.

LEONORA:
Nol posso.

CARLOS:
Fratello! In nome del Signore.

LEONORA:
Nol posso.

CARLOS: *(from within)*
I am dying! Confession! Save my soul.

ALVARO: *(entering with a drawn sword)*
This again is the blood of a Vargas!

CARLOS:
Confession! Confession!

ALVARO: *(throwing aside his sword)*
I am accursed; but nearby is a hermit.
Come quickly, to console a dying man.

LEONORA: *(from within)*
I cannot.

ALVARO:
Brother! In the name of the Lord.

LEONORA:
I cannot.

ALVARO:
È d'uopo.

ALVARO:
You must!

LEONORA:
Aiuto! Aiuto!

LEONORA: *(ringing the bell)*
Help, help!

ALVARO:
Deh, venite.

ALVARO:
Oh come!

LEONORA:
Temerarii, del ciel l'ira fuggite!

LEONORA:
Rash man, flee the wrath of heaven!

ALVARO:
Un donna! Qual voce!
Ah, no, uno spettro!

ALVARO:
A woman! That voice!
Ah, no, a ghost!

LEONORA:
Che miro?

LEONORA: *(recognizing Don Alvaro)*
What do I see!

ALVARO:
Tu, Leonora!

ALVARO:
You! Leonora!

LEONORA:
Egli è ben desso.
Ah, ti riveggo ancora.

LEONORA: *(approaching Don Alvaro)*
It is really him?
I see you once more.

ALVARO:
Lungi, lungi da me; queste mie mani
grondano sangue. Indietro!

ALVARO:
Keep away from me, these hands of mine
are dripping with blood. Stand back!

LEONORA:
Che mai parli?

LEONORA:
What are you saying?

ALVARO:
Là giace spento un uom.

ALVARO:
Over there, there lies a dead man.

LEONORA:
Tu l'uccidesti?

LEONORA:
You killed him?

ALVARO:
Tutto tentai per evitar la pugna.
Chiusi i miei dì nel chiostro.
Eì mi raggiunse, m'insultò, l'uccisi.

ALVARO:
I tried everything to avoid the fight.
I sought to end my days in a monastery.
He found me, insulted me, I killed him.

LEONORA:
Ed era?

LEONORA:
And who was he?

ALVARO:
Tuo fratello!

LEONORA:
Gran Dio!

ALVARO:
Destino avverso,
come a scherno mi prendi!
Vive Leonora, e ritrovarla deggio or che
versai di suo fratello il sangue!

LEONORA:
Ah!

ALVARO:
Qual grido! Che avvene?
Ella, ferita!

LEONORA:
Nell'ora estrema perdonar non seppe.
E l'onta vendicò nel sangue mio.

ALVARO:
E tu paga, non eri, o vendetta di Dio.
Maledizione!

PADRE GUARDIANO:

ALVARO:
Your brother!

LEONORA: (*She rushes to find Carlo)*
Great God!

ALVARO:
Hostile fate,
how you mock me!
Leonora is alive, and I had to find her again
now that I have spilled her brother's blood!

LEONORA:*(crying)*
Ah!

ALVARO: *(Leonora has been wounded)*
What a cry! What has happened?
She is wounded!

LEONORA: *(dying)*
In his final hour he could not forgive,
and he avenged the shame with my blood.

ALVARO:
And you were not to be recompensed,
o God of vengeance! Curses!

FATHER SUPERIOR: *(solemnly)*

Non imprecare; umiliati
a Lui ch' è giusto e santo,
che adduce a eterni gaudii
per una via di pianto;
d'ira e fulgor sacrilego
non profferir parola,
vedi, vedi quest'angiol vola
al trono del Signor.

LEONORA:
Sì, piangi e prega.
Di Dio il perdono io ti prometto.

Do not curse: humble yourself before Him
who is just and holy, who leads us to
eternal joys by a path of tears.
Do not utter a word of anger
or vent sacrilegious fury.
You see, this angel is on her way
to the throne of God.
Kneel!

LEONORA:
Yes, weed and pray.
I promised you God's pardon.

ALVARO:
Un reprobo, un maledetto io sono.
Flutto di sangue innalzasi fra noi.

ALVARO:
I am a reprobate and accursed.
A wave of blood rises between us.

LEONORA:
Piangi! Prega!

LEONORA:
Weep! Pray!

PADRE GUARDIANO:
Prostrati!

FATHER SUPERIOR:
Kneel!

ALVARO:
A quell'accento più non poss'io resistere.
Leonora, io son redento,
dal ciel son perdonato!

ALVARO: *(throwing himself at Leonora)*
I can no longer resist the sound of her voice.
Leonora, I am redeemed,
I am pardoned by heaven !

LEONORA e PADRE GUARDIANO:
Sia lode a Te, Signor.

LEONORA and FATHER SUPERIOR:
Praise be to Thee, Lord!

LEONORA:
Lieta or poss'io precederti
alla promessa terra.
Là cesserà la guerra,
santo l'amor sarà.

LEONORA: *(to Alvaro)*
Praise be to Thee, Lord!
Gladly I can precede you to the promised
land. There, war shall cease,
and love will be sacred.

ALVARO:
Tu mi condanni a vivere.
e m'abbandoni intanto!
Il reo, il reo soltanto
dunque impunito andrà!

ALVARO:
You condemn me to live,
and meanwhile you abandon me!
The guilty one alone
will then go unpunished!

PADRE GUARDIANO:
Santa del suo martirio
ella al Signor ascenda,
e il suo martir t'apprenda
la fede e la pietà!

FATHER SUPERIOR:
Holy in her martyrdom,
she is ascending to the Lord,
and her death
teaches us mercy!

LEONORA:
In ciel ti attendo, addio!

LEONORA:
I await you in heaven. Farewell!

ALVARO:
Deh, non lasciarmi, Leonora, ah no, non
lasciarmi.

ALVARO:
Ah, do not leave me, Leonora,
do not leave me!

LEONORA:
Ah, ti precedo, Alvaro, Ah.
Alvar.....Ah!

LEONORA:
Ah, I precede you, Alvaro.
Ah, Alvar......Ah!

ALVARO:
Morta!

ALVARO:
She is dead!

PADRE GUARDIANO:
Salita a Dio!

FATHER SUPERIOR:
She has risen to God!

END of ACT IV
END of OPERA

Dictionary of Opera and Musical Terms

Accelerando - Play the music faster, but gradually.

Adagio - At a slow or gliding tempo, not as slow as largo, but not as fast as andante.

Agitato - Restless or agitated.

Allegro - At a brisk or lively tempo, faster than andante but not as fast as presto.

Andante - A moderately slow, easy-going tempo.

Appoggiatura - An extra or embellishing note preceding a main melodic note. Usually written as a note of smaller size, it shares the time value of the main note.

Arabesque - Flourishes or fancy patterns usually applying to vocal virtuosity.

Aria - A solo song usually structured in a formal pattern. Arias generally convey reflective and introspective thoughts rather than descriptive action.

Arietta - A shortened form of aria.

Arioso - A musical passage or composition having a mixture of free recitative and metrical song.

Arpeggio - Producing the tones of a chord in succession rather than simultaneously.

Atonal - Music that is not anchored in traditional musical tonality; it does not use the diatonic scale and has no keynote or tonal center.

Ballad opera - Eighteenth-century English opera consisting of spoken dialogue and music derived from popular ballad and folksong sources. The most famous is *The Beggar's Opera,* which is a satire of the Italian opera seria.

Bar - A vertical line across the stave that divides the music into measures.

Baritone - A male singing voice ranging between bass and tenor.

Baroque - A style of artistic expression prevalent in the 17th century that is marked by the use of complex forms, bold ornamentation, and florid decoration. The Baroque period extends from approximately 1600 to 1750 and includes the works of the original creators of modern opera, the Camerata, as well as the later works by Bach and Handel.

Bass - The lowest male voice, usually divided into categories such as:

> **Basso buffo** - A bass voice that specializes in comic roles: Dr. Bartolo in Rossini's *The Barber of Seville.*
>
> **Basso cantante** - A bass voice that demonstrates melodic singing quality: King Philip in Verdi's *Don Carlos.*
>
> **Basso profundo** - the deepest, most profound, or most dramatic of bass voices: Sarastro in Mozart's *The Magic Flute.*

Bel canto - Literally, "beautiful singing." It originated in Italian opera of the 17th and 18th centuries and stressed beautiful tones produced with ease, clarity, purity, and evenness, together with an agile vocal technique and virtuosity. Bel canto flourished in the first half of the 19th century in the works of Rossini, Bellini, and Donizetti.

Cabaletta - A lively, concluding portion of an aria or duet. The term is derived from the Italian word "cavallo," or horse: it metaphorically describes a horse galloping to the finish line.

Cadenza - A flourish or brilliant part of an aria (or concerto) commonly inserted just before a finale. It is usually performed without accompaniment.

Camerata - A gathering of Florentine writers and musicians between 1590 and 1600 who attempted to recreate what they believed was the ancient Greek theatrical synthesis of drama, music, and stage spectacle; their experimentation led to the creation of the early structural forms of modern opera.

Cantabile - An indication that the singer should sing sweetly.

Cantata - A choral piece generally containing Scriptural narrative texts: the *St. Matthew Passion* of Bach.

Cantilena - Literally, "little song." A lyrical melody meant to be played or sung "cantabile," or with sweetness and expression.

Canzone - A short, lyrical operatic song usually containing no narrative association with the drama but rather simply reflecting the character's state of mind: Cherubino's "Voi che sapete" in Mozart's *The Marriage of Figaro.*

Castrato - A young male singer who was surgically castrated to retain his treble voice.

Cavatina - A short aria popular in 18th and 19th century opera that usually heralded the entrance of a principal singer.

Classical Period - A period roughly between the Baroque and Romantic periods, the late 18th through the early 19th centuries. Stylistically, the music of the period stresses clarity, precision, and rigid structural forms.

Coda - A trailer added on by the composer after the music's natural conclusion. The coda serves as a formal closing to the piece.

Coloratura - Literally, "colored": it refers to a soprano singing in the bel canto tradition. It is a singing technique that requires great agility, virtuosity, embellishments and ornamentation: The Queen of the Night's aria, "Zum Leiden bin ich auserkoren," from Mozart's *The Magic Flute*.

Commedia dell'arte - A popular form of dramatic presentation originating in Renaissance Italy in which highly stylized characters were involved in comic plots involving mistaken identities and misunderstandings. Two of the standard characters were Harlequin and Colombine: The "play within a play" in Leoncavallo's *I Pagliacci.*

Comprimario - A singer who performs secondary character roles such as confidantes, servants, and messengers.

Continuo, Basso continuo - A bass part (as for a keyboard or stringed instrument) that was used especially in baroque ensemble music; it consists of an independent succession of bass notes that indicate the required chords and their appropriate harmonies. Also called *figured bass, thoroughbass.*

Contralto - The lowest female voice, derived from "contra" against, and "alto" voice; a voice between the tenor and mezzo-soprano.

Countertenor - A high male voice generally singing within the female high soprano ranges.

Counterpoint - The combination of two or more independent melodies into a single harmonic texture in which each retains its linear character. The most sophisticated form of counterpoint is the fugue form, in which from two to six melodies can be used; the voices are combined, each providing a variation on the basic theme but each retaining its relation to the whole.

Crescendo - A gradual increase in the volume of a musical passage.

Da capo - Literally, "from the top"; repeat. Early 17th-century da capo arias were in the form of A B A, with the second A section repeating the first, but with ornamentation.

Deus ex machina - Literally "god out of a machine." A dramatic technique in which a person or thing appears or is introduced suddenly and unexpectedly; it provides a contrived solution to an apparently insoluble dramatic difficulty.

Diatonic - A major or minor musical scale that comprises intervals of five whole steps and two half steps.

Diminuendo - Gradually becoming softer; the opposite of crescendo.

Dissonance - A mingling of discordant sounds that do not harmonize within the diatonic scale.

Diva - Literally, "goddess"; generally the term refers to a leading female opera star who either possesses, or pretends to possess, great rank.

Dominant - The fifth tone of the diatonic scale; in the key of C, the dominant is G.

Dramatic soprano or tenor - A voice that is powerful, possesses endurance, and is generally projected in a declamatory style.

Dramma giocoso - Literally, "amusing (or humorous) drama." An opera whose story combines both serious and comic elements: Mozart's *Don Giovanni.*

Falsetto - A lighter or "false" voice; an artificially-produced high singing voice that extends above the range of the full voice.

Fioritura - It., "flowering"; a flowering ornamentation or embellishment of the vocal line within an aria.

Forte, fortissimo - Forte (*f*) means loud; mezzo forte (*mf*) is fairly loud; fortissimo (*ff*) is even louder; additional *fff*'s indicate greater degrees of loudness.

Glissando - Literally, "gliding." A rapid sliding up or down the scale.

Grand opera - An opera in which there is no spoken dialogue and the entire text is set to music, frequently treating serious and tragic subjects. Grand opera flourished in France in the 19th century (Meyerbeer); the genre is epic in scale and combines spectacle, large choruses, scenery, and huge orchestras.

Heldentenor - A tenor with a powerful dramatic voice who possesses brilliant top notes and vocal stamina. Heldentenors are well suited to heroic (Wagnerian) roles: Lauritz Melchior in Wagner's *Tristan und Isolde.*

Imbroglio - Literally, "intrigue"; an operatic scene portraying chaos and confusion, with appropriate diverse melodies and rhythms.

Largo or larghetto - Largo indicates a very slow tempo, broad and with dignity. Larghetto is at a slightly faster tempo than largo.

Legato - Literally, "tied" or "bound"; successive tones that are connected smoothly. The opposite of legato is staccato (short and plucked tones.)

Leitmotif - Literally, "leading motive." A musical fragment characterizing a person, thing, feeling, or idea that provides associations when it recurs.

Libretto - Literally, "little book"; the text of an opera.

Lied - A German song; the plural is "lieder." Originally, a German art song of the late 18th century.

Lyric - A voice that is light and delicate.

Maestro - From the Italian "master"; a term of respect to conductors, composers, directors, and great musicians.

Melodrama - Words spoken over music. Melodrama appears in Beethoven's *Fidelio* and flourished during the late 19th century in the operas of Massenet (*Manon* and *Werther*).

Mezza voce - Literally, "medium voice"; singing with medium or half volume. It is sometimes intended as a vocal means to intensify emotion.

Mezzo-soprano - A woman's voice with a range between soprano and contralto.

Obbligato - An accompaniment to a solo or principal melody that is usually played by an important, single instrument.

Octave - A musical interval embracing eight diatonic degrees; from C to C is an octave.

Opera - Literally, "work"; a dramatic or comic play in which music is the primary vehicle that conveys its story.

Opera buffa - Italian comic opera that flourished during the bel canto era. Highlighting the opera buffa genre were buffo characters who were usually basses singing patter songs: Dr. Bartolo in Rossini's *The Barber of Seville*; Dr. Dulcamara in Donizetti's *The Elixir of Love*.

Opéra comique - A French opera characterized by spoken dialogue interspersed between the musical numbers, as opposed to grand opera in which there is no spoken dialogue. Opéra comique subjects can be either comic or tragic.

Operetta, or light opera - Operas that contain comic elements and generally a light romantic plot: Strauss's *Die Fledermaus*, Offenbach's *La Périchole*, and Lehar's *The Merry Widow*. In operettas, there is usually much spoken dialogue, dancing, practical jokes, and mistaken identities.

Oratorio - A lengthy choral work, usually of a religious nature and consisting chiefly of recitatives, arias, and choruses, but performed without action or scenery: Handel's *Messiah.*

Ornamentation - Extra embellishing notes—appoggiaturas, trills, roulades, or cadenzas—that enhance a melodic line.

Overture - The orchestral introduction to a musical dramatic work that sometimes incorporates musical themes within the work. Overtures are instrumental pieces that are generally performed independently of their respective operas in concert.

Parlando - Literally, "speaking"; the imitation of speech while singing, or singing that is almost speaking over the music. Parlando sections are usually short and have minimal orchestral accompaniment.

Patter song - A song with words that are rapidly and quickly delivered. Figaro's "Largo al factotum" in Rossini's *The Barber of Seville* is a patter song.

Pentatonic - A five-note scale. Pentatonic music is most prevalent in Far Eastern countries.

Piano - A performance indication for soft volume.

Pitch - The property of a musical tone that is determined by the frequency of the waves producing it.

Pizzicato - An indication that notes are to be played by plucking the strings instead of stroking the string with the bow.

Polyphony - Literally, "many voices." A style of musical composition in which two or more independent melodies are juxtaposed; counterpoint.

Polytonal - Several tonal schemes used simultaneously.

Portamento - A continuous gliding movement from one tone to another through all the intervening pitches.

Prelude - An orchestral introduction to an act or a whole opera that precedes the opening scene.

Presto, prestissimo - Vigorous, and with the utmost speed.

Prima donna - Literally, "first lady." The female star or principal singer in an opera cast or opera company.

Prologue - A piece sung before the curtain goes up on the opera proper: Tonio's Prologue in Leoncavallo's *I Pagliacci.*

Quaver - An eighth note.

Range - The span of tonal pitch of a particular voice: soprano, mezzo-soprano, contralto, tenor, baritone, and bass.

Recitative - A formal device used to advance the plot. It is usually sung in a rhythmically free vocal style that imitates the natural inflections of speech; it conveys the dialogue and narrative in operas and oratorios. *Secco*, or dry, recitative is accompanied by harpsichord and sometimes with other continuo instruments; *accompagnato* indicates that the recitative is accompanied by the orchestra.

Ritornello - A refrain, or short recurrent instrumental passage between elements of a vocal composition.

Romanza - A solo song that is usually sentimental; it is shorter and less complex than an aria and rarely deals with terror, rage, or anger.

Romantic Period - The Romantic period is usually considered to be between the early 19th and early 20th centuries. Romanticists found inspiration in nature and man. Von Weber's *Der Freischütz* and Beethoven's *Fidelio* (1805) are considered the first German Romantic operas; many of Verdi's operas as well as the early operas of Wagner are also considered Romantic operas.

Roulade - A florid, embellished melody sung to one syllable.

Rubato - An expressive technique, literally meaning "robbed"; it is a fluctuation of tempo within a musical phrase, often against a rhythmically steady accompaniment.

Secco - "Dry"; the type of accompaniment for recitative played by the harpsichord and sometimes continuo instruments.

Semitone - A half step, the smallest distance between two notes. In the key of C, the half steps are from E to F and from B to C.

Serial music - Music based on a series of tones in a chosen pattern without regard for traditional tonality.

Sforzando - Sudden loudness and force; it must stand out from the texture and be emphasized by an accent.

Singspiel - Literally, "song drama." Early German style of opera employing spoken dialogue between songs: Mozart's *The Magic Flute.*

Soprano - The highest range of the female voice ranging from lyric (light and graceful quality) to dramatic (fuller and heavier in tone).

Sotto voce - Literally, "below the voice"; sung softly between a whisper and a quiet conversational tone.

Soubrette - A soprano who sings supporting roles in comic opera: Adele in Strauss's *Die Fledermaus*; Despina in Mozart's *Così fan tutte.*

Spinto - From the Italian "spingere" (to push); a singer with lyric vocal qualities who "pushes" the voice to achieve heavier dramatic qualities.

Sprechstimme - Literally, "speaking voice." The singer half sings a note and half speaks; the declamation sounds like speaking but the duration of pitch makes it seem almost like singing.

Staccato - Short, clipped, detached, rapid articulation; the opposite of legato.

Stretto - Literally, "narrow." A concluding passage performed in a quick tempo to create a musical climax.

Strophe - Strophe is a rhythmic system of repeating lines. A musical setting of a strophic text is characterized by the repetition of the same music for all strophes.

Syncopation - A shifting of the beat forward or back from its usual place in the bar; a temporary displacement of the regular metrical accent in music caused typically by stressing the weak beat.

Supernumerary - A "super"; a performer with a non-singing and non-speaking role: "Spear-carrier."

Symphonic poem - A large orchestral work in one continuous movement, usually narrative or descriptive in character: Franz Liszt's *Les Preludes*; Richard Strauss's *Don Juan, Till Eulenspiegel,* and *Ein Heldenleben.*

Tempo - The speed at which music is performed.

Tenor - The highest natural male voice.

Tessitura - The usual range of a voice part.

Tonality - The organization of all the tones and harmonies of a piece of music in relation to a tonic (the first tone of its scale).

Tone poem - An orchestral piece with a program.

Tonic - The principal tone of the key in which a piece is written. C is the tonic of C major.

Trill - Two adjacent notes rapidly and repeatedly alternated.

Tutti - All together.

Twelve-tone - The twelve chromatic tones of the octave placed in a chosen fixed order and constituting, with some permitted permutations and derivations, the melodic and harmonic material of a serial musical piece. Each note of the chromatic scale is used as part of the melody before any other note is repeated.

Verismo - Literally "truth"; the artistic use of contemporary everyday material in preference to the heroic or legendary in opera. A movement particularly in Italian opera during the late 19th and early 20th centuries: Mascagni's *Cavalleria rusticana.*

Vibrato - A "vibration"; a slightly tremulous effect imparted to vocal or instrumental tone to enrich and intensify sound, and add warmth and expressiveness through slight and rapid variations in pitch.

Opera Journeys™ Mini Guide Series

Opera Journeys™ Libretto Series

Opera Classics Library™ Series

A History of Opera: Milestones and Metamorphoses

Puccini Companion: the Glorious Dozen

Mozart's da Ponte Operas

Fifty Timeless Opera Classics

PUCCINI COMPANION: THE GLORIOUS DOZEN

756-page Soft Cover volume

Each Puccini Chapter features:

COMPLETE LIBRETTO
Italian-English side-by-side

STORY NARRATIVE
with 100s of Music Highlight Examples

ANALYSIS AND COMMENTARY

Print or Ebook

A HISTORY of OPERA: MILESTONES and METAMORPHOSES

432 pages, soft cover / 21 chapters

featuring **0ver 250 music examples**

- A comprehensive survey of milestones in opera history
- All periods are analyzed in depth:

Baroque, Classical, Romantic, Bel Canto, Opera Buffa, German Romanticism, Wagner and music drama, Verismo, plus analyses of the "Tristan Chord," atonalism, minimalism...

Print or Ebook

OPERA JOURNEYS' COLLECTION: FIFTY TIMELESS OPERA CLASSICS

816-page Soft Cover volume

Print or EBook

A collection of fifty of the most popular operas
in the Opera Journeys Mini Guide Series,
each with Story Narrative and 100s of Music Examples,
PLUS insightful,in delpth commentary and analysis

MOZART'S DA PONTE OPERAS:

Don Giovanni, The Marriage of Figaro, Così fan tutte

348-page Soft or Hard Cover Edition

Print or Ebook

Mozart: Master of Musical Characterization;
Da Ponte: Ambassador of Italian Culture.

Featuring: Principal Characters, Brief Story Synopsis, Story Narrative, Music Highlight Examples, and insightful in depth Commentary and Analysis, PLUS a newly translated LIBRETTO of each opera with Italian/English translation side-by-side.

ORDER: Opera Journeys' Web Site www.operajourneys.com

OPERA JOURNEYS LIBRETTO SERIES

Print or Ebook

New translations (side-by-side) with Music Highlight Examples

•Aida •The Barber of Seville •La Bohème
•Carmen •Cavalleria Rusticana •La Cenerentola
•Così fan tutte •Don Carlo •Don Giovanni
•La Fanciulla del West •Gianni Schicchi
•Lucia di Lammermoor •Madama Butterfly
•The Magic Flute •Manon Lescaut
•The Marriage of Figaro •A Masked Ball
•Otello •I Pagliacci •Rigoletto •La Rondine
•Salome Samson and Delilah •Suor Angelica
•Il Tabarro •Tosca •La Traviata •Il Trovatore •Turandot

OPERA JOURNEYS MINI GUIDE SERIES

Print or Ebook

featuring 125 titles

- ***Brief Story Synopsis***
- ***Principal Characters***
- ***Story Narrative***
- ***Music Highlight Examples***
- ***Commentary and Analysis***

•The Abduction from the Seraglio •Adriana Lecouvreur •L'Africaine •Aida •Andrea Chénier
•Anna Bolena •Ariadne auf Naxos •Armida •Attila •The Ballad of Baby Doe •The Barber of Seville
•Duke Bluebeard's Castle •La Bohème •Boris Godunov •Candide •Capriccio •Carmen
•Cavalleria Rusticana •Cendrillon •La Cenerentola •La Clemenza di Tito •Le Comte Ory
•Così fan tutte •The Crucible •La Damnation de Faust •The Death of Klinghoffer •Doctor Atomic
• Don Carlo • Don Giovanni •Don Pasquale •La Donna del Lago •The Elixir of Love •Elektra
•Ernani •Eugene Onegin •Exploring Wagner's Ring •Falstaff •La Fanciulla del West •Faust
•La Fille du Régiment •Fidelio •Die Fledermaus •The Flying Dutchman •Die Frau ohne Schatten
•Der Freischütz •Gianni Schicchi •La Gioconda •Hamlet •Hansel and Gretel •Henry VIII
•Iolanta •L'Italiana in Algeri •Les Huguenots •Iphigénie en Tauride •Julius Caesar •Lakmé
•Lohengrin •Lucia di Lammermoor •Macbeth •Madama Butterfly •The Magic Flute
•The Makropolis Case •Manon •Manon Lescaut •Maria Stuarda •The Marriage of Figaro
•A Masked Ball •Die Meistersinger •The Mikado •Nabucco •Nixon in China •Norma
•Of Mice and Men •Orfeo ed Euridice •Otello •I Pagliacci •Parsifal •The Pearl Fishers
•Pelléas et Mélisande •Porgy and Bess •Prince Igor •I Puritani •The Queen of Spades
•The Rake's Progress •The Rape of Lucretia •The Rhinegold •Rigoletto •The Ring of the Nibelung
•Roberto Devereaux •Rodalinda •Roméo et Juliette •La Rondine •Der Rosenkavalier •Rusalka
•Salome •Samson and Delilah •Show Boat •Siegfried •Simon Boccanegra •La Sonnambula
•Suor Angelica •Susannah •Il Tabarro •The Tales of Hoffmann •Tannhäuser •Thaïs •Tosca
•La Traviata •Tristan and Isolde •Il Trittico •Les Troyens •Il Trovatore •Turandot
•Twilight of the Gods •The Valkyrie •Werther •West Side Story •Wozzeck

ORDER: Opera Journeys' Web Site www.operajourneys.com

37414758R00064

Made in the USA
Middletown, DE
26 February 2019